The Progress of the
AFRO-AMERICAN

By

JOHN J. PATRICK

Illustrated by

MICHAEL DAVIS

BENEFIC PRESS • WESTCHESTER, ILLINOIS

Contents

Library of Congress
Number 68-23044

Historical Documents

Acknowledgment is made to the following for permission to reproduce photographs.

President Kennedy Speaks to the Nation About Civil Rights
    Moral Crisis: The Case for Civil Rights, Minneapolis: Gilbert Publishing Co., 1964.
Happy Negroes Dispute Their Sheriff
    New York Times, August 9, 1964.
A Racist View of Slavery
    Alexander H. Stephens, *A History of the United States: From the Age of Exploration to 1865,* New York: Meridian Books, Inc., 1960.
The UNESCO Statement on Race
    Ashley Montagu, *Statement on Race,* New York: Henry Shuman, Inc., 1951.
Life of a Slave in Maryland
    Frederick Douglass, *Narrative of the Life of Frederick Douglass: An American Slave,* Garden City, New York: Doubleday and Co., Inc., 1963.
Slavery on a Cotton Plantation in Louisiana
    Solomon Northrup, *Twelve Years a Slave,* Auburn, New York: Derby and Miller, 1853.

A Defense of Slavery
    Harvey Wish, ed., *Ante-Bellum,* New York: G. P. Putnam's Sons, 1960.
Slavery on a Virginia Plantation
    Harvey Wish, ed., *The Slave States,* New York: G. P. Putnam's Sons, 1959.
A Negro's Opinion of Reconstruction
    Frederick Douglass, *Life and Times of Frederick Douglass,* Hartford, Connecticut: Park Publishing Co., 1882.
The Freedom of a Freedman
    B. A. Botkin, ed., *Lay My Burden Down: A Folk History of Slavery,* Chicago: University of Chicago Press, 1945.
A Senator Speaks Out Against the Ku Klux Klan
    Richard N. Current, ed., *Reconstruction: 1865–1877,* Englewood Cliffs, New Jersey: Prentice-Hall, Inc., 1965.
A Virginia Negro's Opinion About Freedom
    Richard N. Current, ed., *Reconstruction: 1865-1877,* Englewood Cliffs, New Jersey: Prentice-Hall, Inc., 1965.
The Freedman's Bureau
    Richard N. Current, ed., *Reconstruction: 1865-1877,* Englewood Cliffs, New Jersey: Prentice-Hall, Inc., 1965.

A Negro is Put in His Place
Richard Wright, *Uncle Tom's Children,* New York: Harper Row, 1936.

Negro Life in Alabama
Booker T. Washington, *Up From Slavery,* New York: Doubleday and Co., Inc.

The Ku Klux Klan Terror
Paul M. Angle, ed., *The American Reader,* New York: Rand McNally and Co., 1958.

Separate But Equal
Hubert H. Humphrey, ed., *School Desegregation,* New York: Thomas Y. Crowell Co., 1964.

Negro Migration
Herbert Aptheker, ed., *A Documentary History of the Negro People in the United States,* New York: Citadel Press, 1951.

A Southerner Defends the Segregation System
Richard N. Current, ed., *Reconstruction: 1865-1877,* Englwood Cliffs, New Jersey: Prentice-Hall, Inc., 1965.

Northern Racism
Chicago Committee on Race Relations, *The Negro in Chicago.* Chicago: University of Chicago Press, 1922.

Black Like Me
John Howard Griffin, *Black Like Me,* Boston: Houghton Mifflin, Co., 1960.

The Niagara Movement
Herbert Aptheker, *A Documentary History of the Negro People in the United States,* New York: Citadel Press, 1951.

Separate Means Unequal
Hubert H. Humphrey, ed., *School Desegregation,* New York: Thomas Y. Crowell Co., 1964.

Conflict in the South
Robert Penn Warren, *Segregation: The Inner Conflict in the South,* New York: Random House, 1956.

Letters From Mississippi
Elizabeth Sutherland, ed., *Letters From Mississippi,* New York: McGraw-Hill, Inc., 1966.

The March on Washington
Martin Luther King, Jr., *Why We Can't Wait.* New York: Harper Row, 1964.

Hubert H. Humphrey Speaks Against Segregation
Hubert H. Humphrey, ed., *School Desegregation,* New York: Thomas Y. Crowell Co., 1964.

The Southern Manifesto
Hubert H. Humphrey, ed., *School Desegregation,* New York: Thomas Y. Crowell Co., 1964.

1. Using Historical Methods

Fellow-citizens, we cannot escape history....
The fiery trail through which we pass
will light us down, in honor or dishonor,
to the latest generation.

Abraham Lincoln
Annual Message to Congress
December 1, 1862

Why learn about the Afro-American?

Negro people have played an important part in the story of America. Negroes were part of some of the earliest explorations in America. In 1619, one year before the Mayflower landed at Plymouth, a Dutch ship brought twenty Negroes to Jamestown, Virginia. These were the first of many thousands of Negroes who were to come to America during the next 250 years. Negroes were also among the earliest settlers of the United States.

During the Revolutionary War, about 5,000 Negroes fought in the army and the navy. Since that time Negroes have fought and died for the United States in every war.

Negroes have contributed in many other important ways to the building of the American nation. They have cleared land, worked in factories, and made discoveries in laboratories. Some Negroes have held important public offices. Others have become well-known entertainers, athletes, artists, writers, and scholars.

The story of the Afro-American is full of important lessons about the strong points and the weak points of the American way of life. The Negro people have suffered greatly in America. Their ancestors were brought to this land by force. Most of these people spent their entire lives in slavery. Even after slavery was ended, American Negroes still faced many hardships and problems.

Negroes were kept from getting a good education. They were kept from an equal chance for a good job. This unfair treatment of American Negroes has been one of the weak points of the American way of life. It shows that our nation has not offered equal opportunity at all times to all of its many people.

But the story of the American Negro has not been entirely filled with troubles. After a bloody Civil War, Negro slaves were made forever free. They were given the freedom to speak, write, and work for laws that would give them greater opportunities for education, jobs, and participation in the government. Over the years more and more Americans, both Negro and white, have joined in the struggle for *civil rights*. These are the full rights, duties, and rewards of citizenship in the United States. The result has been a slow but steady progress toward the full enjoyment of democracy and freedom for all Americans.

This struggle for civil rights has also been violent sometimes. The civil disorders and the riots in the cities of the United States have been partially caused by the feeling that little or no progress has been made in gaining civil rights. Thus the struggle for civil rights has been both peaceful and violent. People everywhere are waiting to see if the American dream of freedom and equality will come true for all Americans.

What is the meaning of historical methods?

Learning about the past can be an exciting adventure. It is full of surprises and the thrill of discovery. It is like putting together the pieces of a jigsaw puzzle, finding the answer to a riddle, or solving a mystery. The clues you use to solve a historical riddle or mystery are found in *documents*. A document is a written record of what men have said or done. There are many kinds of documents. A letter from a man to his family, a woman's diary, a newspaper article, a written law, a written speech, a poem, and a novel are examples of written records. These written rec-

President Kennedy delivered his civil rights speech on June 11, 1963.

ords or documents tell us something about the past. For example, a letter from a man to his family might tell about events he has seen, what the land and cities look like, and what news he has heard.

Documents are the raw material for people who write history books. These documents are the most important sources of information. The facts and the ideas you read in history books come from these documents. These documents are called *primary sources*. They are the original or first-hand source of information. History books are called *secondary sources* because they are not the original or first-hand source of historical information.

How can you use historical methods?

You use historical methods when you discover the clues contained in documents and primary sources. These clues help you find out what has happened in the past. You can learn to use these historical methods by working with President John F. Kennedy's speech on page fifteen. This speech is a document that will give you ideas about how Negroes have progressed in America.

The first step in using documents is to find out who wrote the document, when it was written, and where it was written. Finding these facts will give you clues to help you better understand the ideas in the document.

This speech by President Kennedy was given on June 11, 1963. He spoke to the American people over nation-wide radio and television networks. These facts are clues that tell you this speech was probably a matter of great importance to all Americans. These facts also tell you the year 1963 must have been a time of special problems in the affairs of the nation. The contents of the speech are the ideas of President Kennedy about these special problems.

It is important to know who wrote the document. Different people write different records about what happened. This is because they might hate or like different things. These feelings might change the things they do and say. For example, a speech by a man who hated war and violence would be different than a speech by an army general.

Knowing when the document was written makes it possible for you to place the event in *chronological order*. This means placing past events in the order in which they happened. Placing documents in chronological order helps you to discover if there is some kind of connection or relationship between one document and another. For example, President Kennedy's speech of June 11, 1963 came before the passing of the Civil Rights Bill of 1964. Knowing this helps you understand that this speech might have had something to do with getting people to be in favor

Photographs and drawings can also be used as historical documents. This drawing shows President Lincoln reading the Emancipation Proclamation.

of the Civil Rights Bill of 1964.

The second step in using historical methods is to discover the facts and the opinions that are contained in the document.

A *fact* is something you are certain is true. For example, it is a fact that the Los Angeles Dodgers won the World Series of baseball in 1965. There is no doubt about this fact. Everyone is positive that it is true. You can also prove that it is true by talking to people who saw the World Series, or you could look up the information in baseball records.

An *opinion* is a belief or judgment about something. It may be your opinion that the Dodgers were lucky to win the World Series. You can believe strongly that this opinion is true, but you can not prove your belief to someone who does not agree with you. You can not be so positive that you can convince everyone that your opinion is true. The speech by

STATUS OF THE NEGRO IN
THE U. S. TODAY --- AS THE PRESIDENT DESCRIBED IT

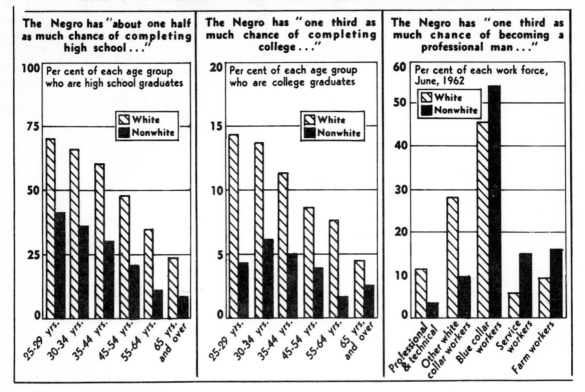

The Negro has "about one half as much chance of completing high school..."

Per cent of each age group who are high school graduates

White
Nonwhite

The Negro has "one third as much chance of completing college..."

Per cent of each age group who are college graduates

White
Nonwhite

The Negro has "one third as much chance of becoming a professional man..."

Per cent of each work force, June, 1962

White
Nonwhite

President Kennedy is full of facts and opinions. For example, President Kennedy said in his speech that American Negroes have one-half as much chance of finishing high school as do American whites. President Kennedy also said that American Negroes have one-third as much chance of finishing college, one-third as much chance of becoming a doctor or lawyer, twice as much chance of not having a job, one-seventh as much chance of earning $10,000 a year, and a life expectancy that is seven years shorter. These are facts that were true at the time President Kennedy made this speech. These facts are shown in the graphs on this page. These graphs are documents that are closely related to President Kennedy's speech. These graphs were taken from the New York Times newspaper of June 16, 1963.

The facts show that most Afro-Americans have had less opportunity than American whites. It was President Kennedy's opinion that this was wrong. It was his opinion that the American people should do something to give Negro people better opportunities to go to school, to get better jobs, to live longer, and to earn more money. It was President Kennedy's opinion also that the United States Congress should pass laws that would open new opportu-

STATUS OF THE NEGRO IN
THE U. S. TODAY---AS THE PRESIDENT DESCRIBED IT.

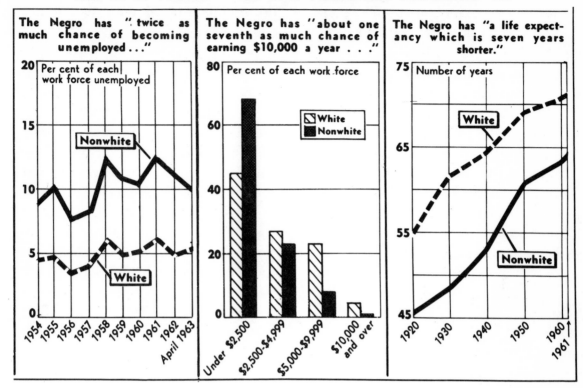

The Negro has ". twice as much chance of becoming unemployed ..."

Per cent of each work force unemployed

Nonwhite

White

1954 1955 1956 1957 1958 1959 1960 1961 1962 April 1963

The Negro has "about one seventh as much chance of earning $10,000 a year ..."

Per cent of each work force

White
Nonwhite

Under $2,500 $2,500-$4,999 $5,000-$9,999 $10,000 and over

The Negro has "a life expectancy which is seven years shorter."

Number of years

White

Nonwhite

1920 1930 1940 1950 1960 1961

---

nities to Afro-Americans. These laws would give Afro-Americans equal opportunities for jobs, equal opportunities for an education, and equal opportunities for housing.

Since documents may be our only source of information about certain past events, it is very important, therefore, to get as many facts as possible from the documents. What are the important facts mentioned in President Kennedy's speech? What are the important opinions mentioned in President Kennedy's speech?

The third step in using documents is to discover why the facts and opinions are important. After finding all of the facts and opinions in a document, you should ask yourself what use you can make of this information. What value does the document have in helping you to understand the past and the present? Do you think the facts given in President Kennedy's speech are important? What questions about American Negroes does this document help you to answer?

The fourth step in learning from documents is to make a *conclusion*. Your conclusion should be your judgment or belief about the question. Do you agree or disagree with the conclusions of President Kennedy? What are your reasons for agreeing or disagreeing?

Your conclusion should be based on the clues given in the document. You should be able to support your conclusion with evidence taken from the document. Find evidence in other documents that helps support your conclusion. You should be able to explain why you think your conclusion is the correct one. The clues given in the Kennedy speech and the graphs from the New York Times should lead you to the conclusion that most American Negro people have had less chance to make progress than have most American white people. This conclusion can be supported by the evidence you have discovered in the two documents. Are there any other conclusions you can make? What are they?

Realize that any conclusions you make may not be absolutely true. They only seem true at the present time. You should be ready to change your conclusion if you find new facts that show your conclusion is wrong.

The fifth step in using historical documents is to ask yourself whether the document raises any new and important questions. Sometimes a document suggests questions that cannot be answered by the facts in the document. For example, there are questions raised by the Kennedy speech that can not be answered by the facts in the document. What caused President Kennedy to speak to the nation about the problems of the Afro-American? Was any action taken to solve the problems of the Afro-American? Why has there been a conflict between American Negroes and whites? What other questions does the speech suggest?

In order to answer these questions, you need to find more facts about the history of the Negro in America. Many of these facts will be found in documents. Many of these facts can be found in the following chapters of this book. Use the historical methods while studying this book.

A Chronology of Civil Rights

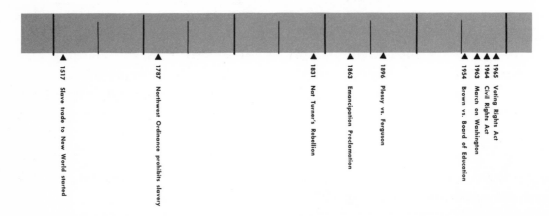

1517 Slave trade to New World started
1787 Northwest Ordinance prohibits slavery
1831 Nat Turner's Rebellion
1863 Emancipation Proclamation
1896 Plessy vs. Ferguson
1954 Brown vs. Board of Education
1963 March on Washington
1964 Civil Rights Act
1965 Voting Rights Act

PRESIDENT KENNEDY SPEAKS TO THE NATION ABOUT CIVIL RIGHTS

Today we are committed to a world wide struggle to promote and protect the rights of all who wish to be free, and when Americans are sent to Viet Nam or West Berlin, we do not ask for whites only. It ought to be possible, therefore, for American students of any color to attend any public institution they select without having to be backed up by troops.

It ought to be possible for American consumers to receive equal service in places of public accommodations, such as hotels and restaurants and theaters and retail stores, without being forced to resort to demonstrations in the streets, and it ought to be possible for American citizens of any color to register and vote in free elections without interference or fear of reprisal.

It ought to be possible in short, for every American to enjoy the privileges of being American without regard to his race or his color. In short, every American ought to have the right to be treated as one would wish his children to be treated. But this is not the case.

The Negro baby born in America today, regardless of the section of the nation in which he is born, has about one-half as much chance of completing high school as a white baby born in the same place on the same day, one-third as much chance of completing college, one-third as much chance of becoming a professional man, twice as much chance of becoming unemployed, about one-seventh as much chance of earning $10,000 a year, a life expectancy which is seven years shorter, and the prospects of earning only half as much.

This is not a sectional issue. Difficulties over segregation and discrimination exist in every city, in every State of the Union, producing in many cities a rising tide of discontent that threatens the public safety. . . . This is not even a legal or legislative issue alone. It is better to settle these matters in the courts than on the streets, and new laws are needed at every level, but law alone cannot make men see right.

We are confronted primarily with a moral issue. It is as old as the scriptures and is as clear as the American Constitution.

The heart of the question is whether all Americans are to be afforded equal rights and opportunities, whether we are going to treat our fellow Americans as we want to be treated. If an American, because his skin is dark, cannot eat lunch in a restaurant open to the public, if he cannot send his children to the best public school available, if he cannot vote for the public officials who represent him, if, in short, he cannot enjoy the full and free life which all of us want, then who among us would be content to have the color of his skin changed and stand in his place? Who among us would then be content with the counsels of patience and delay?

100 years of delay have passed since President Lincoln freed the slaves, yet their heirs, their grandsons, are not fully free. They are not yet freed from the bonds of injustice. They are not yet freed from special and economic oppression, and this Nation for all its hopes and all its boasts, will not be fully free until its citizens are free. . . .

Now the time has come for this Nation to fulfill its promise. . . .

It is time to act in the Congress, in your State and local legislative body, and above all, in all of our daily lives. . . .

I am, therefore, asking Congress to enact legislation giving all Americans the right to be served in facilities which are open to the public—hotels, theaters, retail stores, and similar establishments. . . .

Other features will also be required, including greater protection for the right to vote. But legislation, I repeat, cannot solve this problem alone, it must be solved in the homes of every community across our country. . . .

HAPPY NEGROES DISPUTE THEIR SHERIFF

This document is a newspaper article which appeared in the New York Times on August 9, 1964. It tells what Negroes in Mississippi think about their way of life and the problems they have to overcome.

A Mississippi sheriff's published remark that "95 per cent of our blacks are happy" has led to an unusual Negro reaction in his cotton-growing county.

More than 20 Negro residents of Bolivar County have written or dictated letters to the New York Times to dispute the sheriff. Bolivar County runs along the Mississippi River, starting 100 miles below Memphis.

The letters tell of poor pay for hard work in the cotton fields, too little schooling, and fear of losing jobs in the white-dominated community.

Written by rural people who often have had little education, they contain statements like these:

"The Negroes that says they are doing fine are lying because they are scared of losing their little two cent jobs."

"Only a fool would be happy in Mississippi down here chopping cotton for 30 cents an hour, just think, ten long hours only $3 a day."

"If Capps thinks that we are happy why don't he try living like the Negroes. After he has done this, ask him if he is happy."

"In our schools we don't have the books the white have. We can't get to learn anything. The colored people is afraid to tell you all we is not happy because we're scared of losing the jobs we have. When we go to the gas stations we don't have any bathrooms. We're glad that the white people are coming down from the North and that they are thinking of our welfare. We work 12 hours a day and only get $3 pay. Sure, we're inferior. If we had better schools, better books, things would be different. If we had better jobs and more money we'd be better off and we'd be more intelligent. We could afford to send our children to school."

"We are afraid to speak for our rights, we are afraid to register to vote, afraid of being jailed or beaten."

Using Historical Methods

1. Is the document "Happy Negroes Dispute Their Sheriff" a primary or a secondary source?

2. Place the three documents in this chapter in chronological order. Is there any relationship among the three documents?

3. What are the facts and the opinions given in "Happy Negroes Dispute Their Sheriff?"

4. What conclusions can be made after reading this document from the New York Times?

5. What questions are raised by the comments of the people in the document "Happy Negroes Dispute Their Sheriff?"

6. What would be the sheriff's reasons for his remark in this document from the New York Times?

Knowing Your Vocabulary

civil rights /ˈsiv-əl-rīts/
The full rights, duties, and rewards of citizenship in the United States. 9

document /ˈdäk-yə-ˌment/
A written record of what men have said or done. 10

primary source /ˈprī-ˌmer-ē ˈsō(ə)rs
The original or first-hand source of historical information. 10

secondary source /ˈsek-ən-ˌder-ē ˈsō(ə)rs/
Sources of information that are not the original source. 10

chronological order /ˌkrän-əl- ˈäj-i-kəl ˈȯrd-ər/
Placing past events in the order in which they happened. 11

fact /ˈfakt/
Something you are certain is absolutely true. 12

opinion /ə-ˈpin-yən/
A belief or judgment about something. 12

conclusion /kən-ˈklü-zhən/
Your judgment about a question after studying the facts. 13

Reading the Text

1. What are some of the reasons it is important to study the history of the Afro-American?

2. Why is the historical method used?

3. What is the difference between a fact and an opinion?

4. What questions should you ask yourself as you read a document?

5. What are the five steps that are used in the historical method?

Identifying Names and Places

John F. Kennedy
New York Times
Civil War
Civil Rights Bill of 1964

2. Race and Racism

I am the inferior of any man whose rights I trample underfoot. Men are not superior by reason of the accidents of race or color. They are superior who have the best heart—the best brain. . . .

Robert Green Ingersoll
Liberty

What is racism?

Many white Americans have certain beliefs about Negroes. They believe Negroes are dirty, lazy, and carefree. They believe Negroes are not well-behaved and have less ambition than white people. They believe Negroes are born inferior to white people. How many of you know people who believe these things about Negroes? Are these beliefs facts or opinions? Why are they opinions?

These beliefs have had an important effect upon the progress of American Negroes. These beliefs have been the cause of much trouble for all Americans. White people who believed that Negroes were born inferior saw nothing wrong with holding Negroes as slaves. They concluded that Negroes were not able to properly take care of themselves. They concluded that Negroes were better off as slaves than as free men.

After the end of slavery, these same beliefs led many white people to think laws should be passed to keep Negroes from having equal rights and opportunities. These white people concluded that Negroes did not need equal opportunities to go to school. They felt that too much education would be a waste of time for people who were fit only to be servants, laborers, or workers.

These white people concluded that Negroes did not need equal political rights. They felt that it would be dangerous if Negroes were allowed to vote or were elected to important jobs in government. They felt that Negroes were not smart enough to hold public office.

Finally, they concluded that all Negroes should be kept "in their place." This meant Negroes should serve, respect, and obey all white people. They felt Negroes should be kept separate and apart from white people. They felt Negroes should have a lower standard of living than white people. This would mean that Negroes would always have worse jobs, earn less money, live in worse housing, and have fewer possessions.

This belief in the natural superiority of all people of one race over all people of another race is called *racism*. People who believe in racism are called racists. They use the idea of race in a special and false way. They use the idea of race to support their beliefs that Negroes are inferior to whites. Their conclusion is that Negroes are born with less ability than whites. They say that nothing can ever be done to change this "fact of nature."

Racists try to prove their beliefs by showing that Negroes earn less money than white people, have less education, live in the poorer parts of our towns and cities, commit more crimes, and are less likely to become community or national leaders. Are the racists reaching the correct conclusions from the facts? What is the correct conclusion?

Why is racism a false idea?

Racists reach the conclusion that because most Negroes have lowly jobs and are poor means that Negroes are fit only to have lowly jobs and to be poor. But scientists have shown that racism is a false idea. Scientists say the idea of race can not be used to prove that all Negroes are born inferior to all white people. Scientists say that all racial groups have the same approximate mental capacity and ability.

Racists use the idea of race to explain why many Negroes behave differently than many whites. But scientists have shown that people behave because of what they learn from other people.

The things you learn at home from your parents, at school from your teachers, at church from your ministers, and at play from your friends are the things that shape your behavior. What you learn as a child shapes your behavior for the rest of your life. As a child you learn to speak, read, and write a certain language. You learn to have faith in a religion, to be patriotic to your country, to obey the laws, and to behave in many other ways. You learn all of these ways of behavior from your parents, teachers, and friends. The important thing to remember is that your language, religion, laws, and ways of behavior have nothing to do with your race. Your race does not shape your behavior.

Your behavior is partly shaped by your parents, your friends, and the groups to which you belong.

NEGROES ARE CONCENTRATED IN JOBS WITH LOW WAGE SCALES.

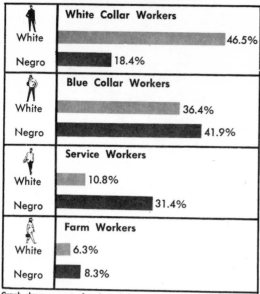

Graph shows percent of each work force

NEGROES ARE PAID LESS THAN WHITES FOR EQUIVALENT WORK.

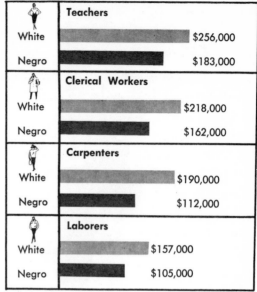

Graph shows life-time earnings

Just because you were born in the United States of America does not mean that you naturally speak the English language. An American is not born with special qualities that make him behave in certain ways. An American learns these ways of behavior. These ways of behavior are different from the behavior of people in other countries. Because these ways of behavior are learned, not inborn, they can be changed through new learning. If an American child is taken to live in another country, he will not learn to behave in the same ways as other Americans. Instead, he will learn the language, religion, laws, and customs of this other country. These new ways of behavior will have been taught to him at school, at home, at work, and at play. He will have learned many new ways of behavior.

American Negroes and whites live in the same country. They have learned to behave alike in many ways. American whites and Negroes have also been separated and lived apart for many years. They have not mixed or been allowed to mix freely and easily with one another. They have learned to behave differently because of this separation. They have learned different customs, beliefs, and ways of acting and speaking.

If Negroes and whites behave in different ways, this has nothing to do with race. The explanation for these differences in behavior is a difference in learning. American Negroes and whites have learned different ways of thinking, behaving, and speaking. They have learned these different ways of behaving because they have been separated from each other for many years.

21

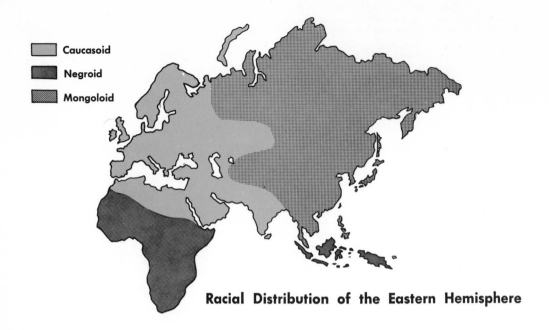

Racial Distribution of the Eastern Hemisphere

- Caucasoid
- Negroid
- Mongoloid

Studying the history of the Afro-American can help you learn the similarities and the differences in behavior between American Negroes and white people. Studying the history of the Afro-American will also help you understand the causes of these differences. As you study you will find that the idea of race has nothing to do with a person's behavior. Behavior is learned and can be changed. The mistake of racists in America is their idea that behavior is due to race. They say the behavior of Negro people is different from the behavior of white people. Racists say Negroes were born to behave in certain ways. Scientists have shown this idea to be false. Scientists have shown that no one race is superior.

How can you use the idea of race correctly?

The idea of race should be used to understand the physical or bodily differences among people. Among these differences are the color of the skin, the color of the eyes, the shape of the head, and the shape of the nose and lips.

Most scientists have divided the people of the world into three main races. These three main racial groups are the *Mongoloid*, the *Caucasoid*, and the *Negroid*. People that are part of one racial group have similar physical features. For example, all Mongoloids have certain similar features. These features make them look like one another and different from people of other racial groups.

What are the differences in the races of man?

The differences among the races of man probably arose over a period of many thousands of years. There were many groups of early men who *migrated* or moved from one area of the earth to another area. After each group had migrated, they developed different physical features. This was because the body of each person had to make certain changes to fit his new surroundings. His body would change if he migrated to a different climate. These changes have developed into the physical differences that we see today among the races of man.

The largest or most numerous of the three races is the Mongoloid. People of this race probably devel-oped in Asia, north and east of the Himalaya Mountains. The Mongo-loids have skin tending to be yellow or cream colored. These people usu-ally have straight black hair and dark eyes. One group of Mongoloids crossed the land bridge that con-nected northeastern Asia with North America. From this migration devel-oped the American Indians.

The second largest group of the races is the Caucasoid. This race has a skin color that varies from white to a rather dark tan. This race prob-ably developed in central Asia, then migrated to India and northern Asia. Afterwards, this race migrated to Europe, and from Europe many Cau-casoid people migrated to North and South America.

These three boys from different parts of the world display certain characteristics common to the three main racial groups.

Caucasoid-Mongoloid   Ainu — Japan

Negroid-Mongoloid   Bushman
Kalahari

Around the Mediterranean Sea and in India, people tend to have a darker skin coloring than those farther north, but their other characteristics remained typically Caucasoid. Hair and eye color were generally lighter among the tribes who roamed throughout northern Europe and the plateaus of central and northern Asia.

The least numerous of the three main racial groups is the Negroid.

This race probably first developed in the southern lands of Asia and Africa. The people of this race have a dark skin coloring, dark eyes, and tightly curled hair.

Today there are no pure races. There are, however, many mixtures or combinations of these three main racial groups. Many sub-races have developed from these combinations of the races. There is a great variety of races today.

24

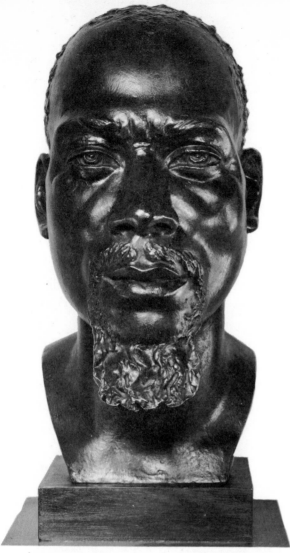

Negroid-Caucasoid   Dahomey Man

American Negroes belong to which racial group?

American Negroes are part of the Negroid racial group. Most of the people living in central and southern Africa are also part of the Negroid group. Some of the physical features that Negroids have in common are brown or black skin color, tightly curled head hair, a broad and flat nose shape, and thick lips. These physical features give most Negroid people an appearance that is differ-ent from the appearance of Mongo-loid or Caucasoid people.

Look at the pictures of the three boys on page twenty-three. The physical features of each boy show that he is a member of a certain ra-cial group. The features of each racial group make that group appear differ-ent from other racial groups.

An important idea to remember is that physical features have nothing to do with behavior. Negroids in Africa and America may look alike, but their behavior is very different. They speak different languages, wear different clothes, have different be-liefs, and obey different laws. There is a much greater similarity in the behavior of an American Negro and an American white person than there is between an American Negro and an African.

The physical features within any one racial group vary a great deal. Only a few people of any group have all of the features of that group. Some Negroes have darker skin than others. The shape of the nose and lips differ greatly from one person to another. These same differences may be seen among people of the Mongo-loid and the Caucasoid races. This is because there are no pure races. All the races of the world have married and mixed with one another. There are Negroid-Caucasoid, Mongoloid-Caucasoid and Negroid-Mongoloid sub-races scattered in many different regions of the world.

Although these two men have some common characteristics, their beliefs, languages, customs, and behavior are very different.

The physical differences that separate people into different races are less important than the similarities that unite all people. The scientists tell us that all men are brothers. All people, regardless of race, are part of the same human race.

Men of all races have the same kind of body that works in the same way. All men have a four-chambered heart. All men have a skeleton with the same kind and the same number of bones. All men have a brain that gives them the power to think. No one race is superior to another. All races are equal in their abilities. History shows that all races have contributed to human progress. All races have helped the human race advance toward civilization.

The facts from Chapter One show that most American Negroes earn less money, have poorer health, and have less education than American white people. Negroes are not born with a tendency to behave in these ways. The reason why most Afro-Americans have found it difficult to make progress is because they have not had an equal opportunity to go to school, to earn money, or to go to a doctor.

As a group, Afro-Americans have been denied equal rights throughout American history. Racism is an important cause of this denial of equal rights. With the end of racism, progress will come for all Americans of all races.

A RACIST VIEW OF SLAVERY

Alexander H. Stephens became Vice-President of the Confederate States of America in 1861. He decided to explain to the world why he and his government favored Negro slavery.

Our new government is founded . . . upon the great truth that the Negro is not equal to the white man; that slavery—subordination to the superior race—is his natural and normal condition. . . .

. . . the anti-slavery fanatics . . . assume that the Negro is equal, and hence conclude that he is entitled to equal privileges and rights with white men . . . but their premise being wrong, their whole argument fails. . . .

With us, all of the white race, however high or low, rich or poor, are equal in the eye of the law. Not so with the Negro. Subordination is his place. He, by nature . . . is fitted for that condition which he occupies in our system. . . . By experience we know that it is best, not only for the superior, but for the inferior race, that it should be so.

THE UNESCO STATEMENT ON RACE

The United Nations Educational, Scientific, and Cultural Organization issued to the world a statement about race in order to clear up confusion about this idea. This statement was written and approved in 1950 by a group of leading scientists.

Scientists have reached general agreement in recognizing that mankind is one . . .

Likenesses among men are far greater than their differences. . . .

Whenever it has been possible to make allowances for differences in environmental opportunities, tests have shown essential similarity in mental characteristics among all human groups. In short, given similar degrees of cultural opportunity to realize their potentialities, the average achievement of the members of each ethnic group is about the same. . . .

As for personality and character, these may be considered raceless. In every human group a rich variety of personality and character types will be found, and there is no reason for believing that any human group is richer than any other in these respects. . .

According to present knowledge there is no proof that the groups of mankind differ in their innate mental characteristics, whether in respect of intelligence or temperment. The scientific evidence indicates that the range of mental capacities in all ethnic groups is much the same . . .

Lastly, biological studies lend support to the ethic of universal brotherhood, for man is born with drives toward co-operation, and unless these drives are satisfied, men and nations alike fall ill. . . . In this sense every man is his brother's keeper. For every man is a piece of the continent, a part of the main, because he is involved in mankind.

Using Historical Methods

1. What questions are raised by the UNESCO document on race?

2. Compare the graph on page twenty-one with the graphs on pages twelve and thirteen. In what ways are they similar? In what ways are they different?

3. Can the photographs of members of the different racial groups be considered documents?

4. Are the racist ideas facts or opinions?

5. Give an argument for and against each of the racist ideas.

6. What are the facts and the opinions in the document by Alexander Stephens?

7. What are the facts and the opinions in the document by UNESCO?

8. Compare the two documents in this chapter. In what ways are they different?

Knowing Your Vocabulary

racism /ˈrā-ˌsiz-əm/
A belief in the natural superiority of one race over all other races. 19

Mongoloid /ˈmäŋ-gə-ˌlȯid/
One of the three main racial groups in the world. 22

Caucasoid /ˈkȯ-kə-ˌsȯid/
One of the three main racial groups in the world. 22

Negroid /ˈnē-ˌgrȯid/
One of the three main racial groups in the world. 22

migrate /ˈmī-ˌgrāt/
When a group of people move to another area of the earth. 23

Reading the Text

1. Which racist beliefs have not allowed Negroes to have equal opportunities in America?

2. From whom does a person learn behavior?

3. What is meant when a person says that a Negro should be "kept in his place?"

4. How can behavior be changed?

5. What special qualities does a natural born American have?

6. What special qualities are learned by Americans?

7. What is the explanation why American Negroes and whites behave differently?

8. What are the major physical characteristics of the three main races?

2. What are some of the main racist ideas? What is a scientific argument against each of these racist ideas?

Identifying Names and Places

Mongoloid
Caucasoid
Negroid
racism
UNESCO
Alexander Stephens

Reading Other Sources

Bibby, Cyril, *Race, Prejudice, and Education*, New York: Praeger, 1960.

Bontemps, Arna, *Story of the Negro*, New York: Knopf, 1958.

Hughes, Langston and Meltzer, Milton, *A Pictorial History of the Negro in America*, New York: Crown, 1950.

Mason, Philip, *Common Sense About Race*, New York: Macmillan, 1961.

Spangler, Earl, *The Negro in America*, Minneapolis: Lerner, 1966.

Young, Margaret B., *The First Book of American Negroes*, New York: Watts, 1966.

Debating and Discussing Ideas

1. Arrange a class debate. Have one side support the arguments of Alexander Stephens. Have the other side support the arguments of UNESCO.

3. The Era of Slavery

*If you put a chain
around the neck of a slave,
the other end
fastens itself around your own.*

Ralph Waldo Emerson
Self-Reliance

What is slavery?

Have you ever thought how it would feel to lose your freedom? You would be told how to live. You would be under the control of someone else. You would not be paid for any work you do. You would have no rights as a human being. You would have no protection by the law.

As children you are guided and controlled by your parents and teachers. You are told that you can not do certain things until you grow up. But even the strictest parents and teachers can not take away certain rights from you. In the United States there are laws that say no one can take away your right to live. No one can take away your right to go to school, to attend church, or to improve your life.

In the long history of man, many millions of people have known how it feels to have no freedom, to have no rights, and to be completely under the control of other people. These people were called *slaves*.

Slavery has existed among all peoples of the world. The rulers of ancient Egypt used slaves to build their great pyramids. They used slaves to build their houses and temples, to farm their land, and to carry them from place to place when they traveled.

The citizens of ancient Greece and Rome used slaves to do many types of work for them. This freed the slave owners to take part in government affairs, education, and war.

Among the Greeks and Romans, most slaves were European people who had been defeated in battle. But some of the slaves were from Asia and Africa. Later the rulers of the Arabian and Turkish empires held many slaves. These slaves were Europeans, Africans, and Asians.

The rulers of some of the ancient African kingdoms also took slaves. These slaves usually were people who had been defeated in battles. After Europeans started coming to western Africa, these rulers and chiefs would sell their slaves to the European traders. If the European traders could not buy enough slaves, they would raid a village and capture the slaves they needed. Millions of Negro people were brought to North and South America as slaves. This slavery lasted for over two hundred years.

Today slavery is against the law in almost every part of the world. The United Nations has declared that slavery is against the basic rights that every man should enjoy.

The United States outlawed slavery in 1865. This was at the end of a long and bloody civil war. The U.S. was one of the last nations in the world to outlaw slavery. But the fact that Negro slavery was practiced in America helps to explain why American Negroes have had difficulty making progress. The history of slavery explains many problems faced by Afro - Americans in the United States today.

How did Negro slavery begin in America?

Twenty Negroes arrived in Jamestown, Virginia, in 1619. This was twelve years after this colony had been started by the English. This was one year before the "Mayflower" arrived at Plymouth, Massachusetts.

These twenty Negroes were brought from the west coast of Africa on board a Dutch trading ship. They were the first Negroes to settle in North America. They were not, however, the first Negroes to come to the New World. During the 1500's the Spanish and Portuguese traders and explorers had Negroes in their crews. Some of these Negroes traveled to America with explorers such as Balboa in Central America and Cabeza de Vaca in Paraguay, Brazil, and the southwestern United States.

Other Negroes were captured or bought in Africa and taken to the Spanish and Portuguese colonies in America. In the Spanish and the Portuguese colonies, these Negroes worked as slaves. By the time the English settled Jamestown in 1607, there were already many thousands of Negro people living in the Spanish and Portuguese colonies of South and Central America.

The people of Jamestown treated these newly arrived Negroes as *indentured servants*. This meant they had to work for a master for a certain number of years. After they worked for this period of time, they were free. The work they did paid for their ship passage to America. Many Europeans also worked as indentured servants under these exact same conditions.

When slave traders could not buy enough slaves, they would often raid African villages to capture more slaves.

One of these first twenty Negroes became a free man after working two years as an indentured servant. He was Anthony Johnson. His son was the first Negro child in North America to be baptized a Christian. Johnson owned his own plantation and had Negro servants working for him. A few other Negroes also earned their freedom and became plantation owners. Some even had white indentured servants.

Several other shiploads of Negro people were brought to North America by Dutch and English traders during the years 1620 to 1650. Usually these newcomers were made welcome because there was a great need of men to do the hard work of clearing land and building settlements. By 1650 the Negro population of Virginia had increased to three hundred people. A few hundred Negroes lived in Maryland and some of the other English colonies in North America.

The way of life of all Negroes in North America changed greatly in 1661. This was the date when the colony of Virginia made Negro slavery legal. The colony of Maryland passed a slavery law in 1664. Soon all of the English colonies had laws that said Negroes could legally be kept as slaves.

Most Negroes who were free at the time of the slavery laws were allowed to remain free. Even free Negroes suffered insults and bad treatment because of these slavery laws. Many white people thought that all Negroes should be slaves. One reason for the slavery laws was the great need for cheap labor in the colonies. Slavery was the cheapest way to get labor. This need for cheap labor helped to establish slavery in America.

Europeans would lead their newly captured slaves to the coast where ships waited to take the Africans to the New World and to slavery.

Attempts were made to enslave the Indians, but they were not good plantation workers. Indian men were accustomed to a life of fishing and hunting. Women were required to do all the heavy work in the Indian villages. Indian men could not adjust to the settled and routine work of a slave laborer. Either the Indians refused to work, even under the penalty of death, or they did their work so poorly that the slave owners did not want to keep them. Also, Indians had almost no resistance to the diseases of the white man. Illnesses such as measles or the common cold killed the Indians in great numbers. Many Indians died from diseases during their first months in slavery. Plantation owners finally gave up their attempts to enslave the Indians.

African Negroes were able to adjust to the conditions of slavery in America. Many of them had lived a civilized life in their homelands. In Africa they had worked on farms and lived in settled villages or towns. The Africans had been in contact with Europeans a long time and were not so likely to die from diseases. African men were not ashamed to do heavy work. Finally, African Negroes were not as likely to run away as were the Indians. Unlike the Indians, they were in a completely strange land. Unlike the white indentured servants, their skin color made it difficult for runaway slaves to hide from their masters. The Negro's dark skin color soon became a mark or badge of slavery. Negroes were identified only as slaves.

On board ship for the Middle Passage, conditions were crowded, dirty, and horrible. Thousands of Africans died from disease and starvation on board ship.

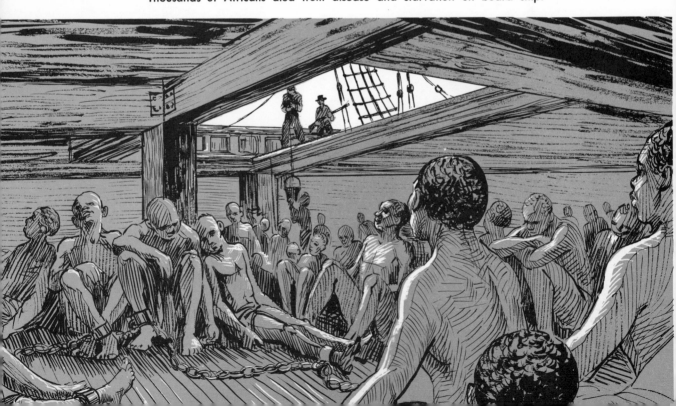

The Negro slavery laws led to a vast trade in human beings between North America and West Africa. This trade was a well established business because it had been going on for over one hundred years between West Africa and South America. Slave traders would come to West Africa with goods to give to African chiefs in exchange for slaves. Many of these slaves were people who had been captured in warfare. But some slave traders brought soldiers with them and raided African villages to kidnap people for slaves.

The traders packed their human cargo into the holds of their ships. This began the horrible *Middle Passage*. This was the name given for the crossing of the Atlantic Ocean by slave ships. Never in the history of sea travel has there been such a terrible trip as the Middle Passage.

Many slaves died from the dirt and the filth aboard the ships. Others died from diseases and starvation. Others killed themselves rather than remain slaves. On their arrival in America, the slaves were unloaded and sold at public auctions to the highest bidder. Many slaves were sold in the West Indies and later resold in the English colonies.

Due to this slave trade, the Negro population of the English colonies increased from a few hundred in the 1650's to almost 60,000 in 1715. By 1808 about 350,000 slaves had been brought to the United States. In 1860, on the eve of the Civil War, almost four and one-half million Negro people lived in the United States of America. Of these four and one-half million Negro people living in America only 500,000 of these Negroes were free.

TRIANGULAR SLAVE TRADE

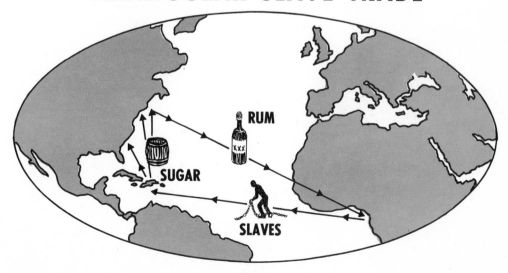

POPULATION OF THE UNITED STATES, 1790-1860			
YEAR	SLAVE	FREE NEGRO	FREE WHITE
1790	697,631	59,577	3,172,006
1800	893,602	108,435	4,306,446
1810	1,191,362	186,446	5,862,073
1820	1,538,022	233,634	7,866,797
1830	2,009,043	319,599	10,537,378
1840	2,487,355	386,293	14,195,805
1850	3,204,313	434,495	19,553,068
1860	3,953,760	488,070	26,922,537

Why did slavery become so important to the South?

Before 1800 slavery existed in all of the states of the United States. After 1800 slavery was practiced only in the South. All of the northern states had passed laws against slavery. The reason why the northern states made slavery illegal was they did not need slaves. The slave system was not suited to northern factories. Immigrants from Europe settled in the North and worked at the jobs available in the factories. Northern farmers grew their own crops on their small or medium sized farms.

Conditions were different in the South. Much farming was done on large plantations. These plantations were hundreds or even thousands of acres in size. They were owned by rich and important men called *planters*. The planters used slave labor to grow crops such as cotton and tobacco. They felt that a low-cost supply of labor, such as slaves, was necessary if they were to make a large profit. The more cotton and tobacco they could grow, the more money they would make. The more money they made, the more slaves they could buy. The more slaves they owned, the more cotton and tobacco they could grow.

Eli Whitney invented the *cotton gin* in 1793. This invention made slavery on the plantation even more important than before. Huge amounts of cotton were needed to keep the machine in operation.

The cotton gin was a machine that separated the seeds from the cotton fibers. But there was no machine to pick cotton. More and more slaves were needed to pick cotton that was needed. Planters needed more and more slaves to clear more land in order to plant more cotton. Both the planting of the cotton and the trading of slaves were the most important businesses in the South. Cotton was king.

Although most southern planters and farmers grew cotton, only about one out of every four people in the South owned slaves in 1860. The vast majority of the white farmers in the South were too poor to buy or own slaves. Many of these poor white farmers hoped for the day when they too could join the planter class and own slaves. They envied the planters who owned hundreds of slaves.

Most of the slave owners owned two to four slaves. They owned small farms rather than large plantations. The majority of farmers grew regular food crops in addition to cotton.

In 1860 only 2,000 planters owned one hundred or more slaves. These were the rich plantation owners. They were the strongest supporters of the slavery system. Their way of life and their riches depended upon the system of slavery as practiced in the South. Even though few in number, these wealthy plantation owners were the most important leaders in the South. They had the most power of any group of people. They influenced the state governments to support slavery laws. They wrote books to convince people that slavery was good for the Negroes. They set the standards of correct behavior and thought in the South.

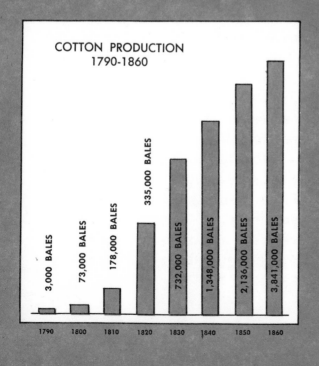

COTTON PRODUCTION
1790-1860

3,000 BALES — 1790
73,000 BALES — 1800
178,000 BALES — 1810
335,000 BALES — 1820
732,000 BALES — 1830
1,348,000 BALES — 1840
2,136,000 BALES — 1850
3,841,000 BALES — 1860

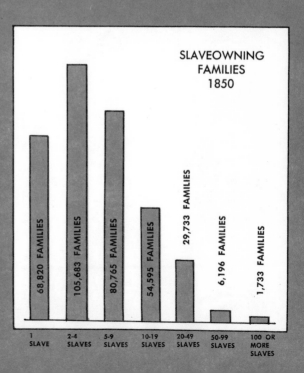

SLAVEOWNING
FAMILIES
1850

68,820 FAMILIES — 1 SLAVE
105,683 FAMILIES — 2-4 SLAVES
80,765 FAMILIES — 5-9 SLAVES
54,595 FAMILIES — 10-19 SLAVES
29,733 FAMILIES — 20-49 SLAVES
6,196 FAMILIES — 50-99 SLAVES
1,733 FAMILIES — 100 OR MORE SLAVES

The work of a slave was never done. He had to work all day in the fields, then return to the plantation and do repairs.

How did Negro slaves live?

There was a wide variety of living conditions for Negro slaves. Some were almost comfortable. Most were miserable. *House slaves* lived better than *field slaves*. The house slaves worked and sometimes lived in the homes of their masters. They were servants, gardeners, housekeepers, and cooks. A few slaves lived in towns and worked as laborers on construction projects or as skilled workers. The field slaves were the largest group. They did all the heavy farm work. The living quarters of the field slaves were usually small wooden shacks. These slave shacks had no windows, no doors, no floors, and little furniture.

The cotton plantation or farm was the usual place of work for a slave. Many slaves also worked on tobacco, rice, and sugar plantations. The day's work began at dawn and lasted until sunset. At certain times of the year, the slaves worked into the night.

The slaves worked in gangs which were bossed by the owner or an *overseer*. The overseer was a man hired to be the boss of a group of slaves. Each gang of slaves usually had its own leader. This leader followed the general instructions of the overseer and told the other slaves what work they were to do that day. Clearing fields, planting cotton, tending the growing plants, and picking cotton were the main jobs of the slaves. It was heavy and very difficult work.

Slaves also had other duties. They mended fences, carried water, chopped wood, and cared for the animals. Slaves worked for little or no reward. They did not want to be slaves. Often the owners and overseers had to force slaves to work. Frequently slaves were beaten or whipped to get more work out of them. It was rare, however, when a slave was killed or severely injured by the owner. This was because a slave represented a large investment or purchase. The owner did not want to lose this large amount of money. By 1860 a young, healthy, male slave cost anywhere from $1,000 to $1,500. Because slaves would do as little work as possible in order to resist their owners, the owners had to buy more and more slaves.

There were laws that limited or restricted the freedom of the slaves. These laws were meant to keep discipline among the slaves and to protect the white owners against slave uprisings and rebellions. Slaves were not allowed to leave their plantation without permission. Slave owners had regular patrols to ride around the countryside looking for Negroes who had escaped from their owners. Slaves could not have guns or firearms. They could not buy or sell goods, they could not own property, and they could not hire themselves out for work. They could not visit the homes of whites or free Negroes, and they were never to gather in a group unless a white person was present. These laws severely limited the freedom of all Negroes.

One of the best ways to resist slavery was to run away. Thousands of slaves ran away from their owners to seek freedom in the North.

Perhaps the worst feature of slavery was the separation of the families. Often husbands and wives were sold to different masters. Many times the children of a family were all sold to different owners. When this happened, the separated members of the family never saw one another again.

The life of a slave depended upon the wishes and the character of the owner. Some owners were very cruel and treated their slaves badly. They worked their slaves hard, fed them poorly, housed them in shacks, and whipped them. The life of a slave was always filled with fear.

How did slaves protest against slavery?

Most slaves were unhappy. Even most of the well taken care of slaves longed for freedom. They wanted to make their own decisions and their own choices in life. Slaves who had cruel masters looked forward to escaping. Many of these slaves also wished to seek revenge against their cruel masters. This unhappiness, hatred, and revenge led many slaves to protest against slavery. They protested in every way they could. Most of them protested by doing as little work as possible. This caused the master to lose money.

Revolt and rebellion against the owners was a bloody way to gain revenge and freedom. Many thousands, however, tried to revolt. From 1650 to 1865, there were over two hundred reported slave revolts. The best known slave revolts were led by Gabriel Prosser, Charles Deslondes, Denmark Vessey, and Nat Turner.

Nat Turner issues orders during what was the bloodiest slave rebellion in the United States.

A newspaper account tells about the Nat Turner rebellion in Southampton County.

SLAVERY RECORD.

INSURRECTION IN VIRGINIA!

Extract of a letter from a gentleman to his friend in Baltimore, dated

'Richmond,' August 23d.

An express reached the governor this morning, informing him that an insurrection had broken out in Southampton, and that, by the last accounts, there were seventy whites massacred, and the militia retreating. Another express to Petersburg says that the blacks were continuing their destruction; that three hundred militia were retreating in a body, before six or eight hundred blacks. A shower of rain coming up as the militia were making an attack, wet the powder so much that they were compelled to retreat, being armed only with shot-guns. The negroes are armed with muskets, scythes, axes, &c. &c. Our volunteers are marching to the scene of action. A troop of cavalry left at four o'clock, P. M. The artillery, with four field pieces, start in the steam boat Norfolk, at 6 o'clock, to land at Smithfield. Southampton county lies 80 miles south of us, below Petersburg.'

From the Richmond Whig, of Tuesday.

Disagreeable rumors have reached this city of an insurrection of the slaves in Southampton County, with loss of life. In order to correct exaggeration, and at the same time to induce all salutary caution, we state the following particulars:

VOL. I.]   WILLIAM LLOYD GARRISON AND ISAAC KNAPP, PUBLISHERS.   [NO. 24.

BOSTON, MASSACHUSETTS.]   OUR COUNTRY IS THE WORLD—OUR COUNTRYMEN ARE MANKIND.   [SATURDAY, JUNE 11, 1831.

"The Liberator" was the most famous abolitionist newspaper. It was published by William Lloyd Garrison and Isaac Knapp.

Gabriel Prosser, a slave in Henrico County, Virginia, secretly planned and organized a revolt in 1800. For months he and his helpers gathered clubs, swords, and knives. Word of this revolt spread from plantation to plantation among the slaves. Prosser started his revolt on August 30, 1800. He and 1,000 other slaves met in a field six miles outside Richmond, Virginia. This band of slaves planned to capture Richmond and to declare themselves free. Prosser began to lead the march on Richmond. A terrible storm started. It halted the march. In the meantime, the whites had learned about the rebellion. Governor James Monroe called up the state *militia* or army. The militia broke up the revolt and captured about one hundred slaves. Prosser and thirty-five of his followers were executed for their part in the slave rebellion.

On January 8, 1811, Charles Deslondes, a free Negro, led a revolt of four hundred slaves in Louisiana. The slaves killed or wounded several white men and destroyed a few plantations. The governor of Louisiana called out five hundred soldiers of the state militia to put down the rebellion. On January 10, 1811, these troops attacked the slaves and killed or captured most of them.

Denmark Vessey was a free Negro carpenter in Charleston, South Carolina. Vessey hated the system that kept thousands of Negroes in slavery. He planned a huge slave uprising. For several years prior to 1822, he made plans, made and collected weapons, and secretly spread word of the revolt to all the slaves in the surrounding countryside. It is suspected that as many as 9,000 slaves were part of this plot to revolt.

41

Vessey's plan was to capture Charleston on the second Sunday in July, 1822. The plan was betrayed to the whites and the state militia was called. Vessey and hundreds of others were arrested before the revolt could take place. Vessey and forty-seven others were hanged for their part in the plot.

The bloodiest slave revolt was in August, 1831. The uprising began when Nat Turner and six other slaves killed their master and his family in Southampton County, Virginia. Turner and his followers began marching across the countryside. They killed all the whites they met. They set free any Negro slaves they found. Within twenty-four hours, sixty whites had been killed and Turner's followers numbered seventy Negroes. The United States Army was called out to stop the revolt. In a battle with Turner and his group, the army killed over one hundred Negroes. Turner escaped and fled. He was captured two months later and was hanged.

What was the Abolition Movement?

Many free Negroes protested against the slavery system by working in the *Abolition Movement*. Abolitionists were people who wanted to do away with slavery. Most Abolitionist lived in the northern states. Southerners who thought slavery was wrong often were forced to leave their homes and live in the North. The members of the Abolition Movement were, therefore, both white and Negro, northerner and southerner.

One of the worst features of slavery was the destruction and breakup of the family. Members of the same family were often auctioned off to separate buyers.

William Lloyd Garrison was perhaps the most famous Abolitionist leader. He was a fiery writer and public speaker for the Abolition Movement. He started *The Liberator*, an outstanding anti-slavery newspaper. He also was a leader of the American Anti-Slavery Society. Garrison and other Abolitionists traveled around the country speaking and writing against the slavery system. They helped free Negroes become educated and find jobs. They helped thousands of slaves run away from their masters.

Famous Negroes in the Abolition Movement were Frederick Douglass, Samuel Cornish, John Russwurm, Sojourner Truth, and Harriet Tubman. These Negro Abolitionists worked tirelessly to convince all Americans that slavery should be ended. They joined with Garrison and other white people to speak and to write against slavery.

The Negro Abolitionists were very active leaders of the *Underground Railroad*. This was the name given to the many escape routes that slaves used to flee from the South into free territory. Many routes of the Underground Railroad went all the way from the Deep South into Canada. The Underground Railroad was very well organized. Many people, Negro and white, northerner and southerner, worked together to help slaves escape. They then helped slaves find jobs, houses, friends, and to settle in the North.

The final result of slavery was rebellion and violence. There were about two hundred reported slave revolts in the United States.

43

Harriet Tubman, far
right, helped this group
of slaves escape from
the South.

These fugitives from slavery usually traveled at night on the Underground Railroad. During the day they rested at the homes of free Negroes or friendly white people. These homes where the fugitives rested were called "stations" on the Underground Railroad. Usually the runaway slaves walked, but they were sometimes carried as freight or cargo in wagons or on trains.

Travel along the routes of the Underground Railroad was dangerous. Usually a "conductor" from the North came to the South to help lead the slaves to freedom. Slave owners organized search parties to hunt down the escaping slaves. All of the southern states had laws against helping a slave escape. These conductors faced large punishments if they were caught. After 1850, the federal

Fugitive Slave Law gave slave owners the right to enter free territory to capture their runaway slaves. After this law, many slaves fled all the way to Canada to be completely safe from their former owners. They would not again become slaves.

Many white people also worked on the Underground Railroad. Of these workers, Levi Coffin and John Fairfield were especially outstanding. Coffin had lived in North Carolina. He moved to Indiana so he could more freely carry on his work in the Abolition Movement and the Underground Railroad. His home in Newport, Indiana, became a favorite station on the Underground Railroad. It is estimated that Levi Coffin helped more than 3,000 slaves escape from the South. Some of these slaves went all the way to Canada.

John Fairfield was the son of a Virginia slave owner. John Fairfield came to hate slavery and moved to the North. Later he became an expert at helping Negroes to escape. Free Negroes in the North would give him descriptions of their friends or relatives in the South, and Fairfield would travel to the South to find these people and lead them to freedom. On some trips he helped as many as twenty slaves to escape.

Harriet Tubman, Elijah Anderson, and John Mason were important Negro conductors on the Underground Railroad. In seven years, from 1848 to 1855, Anderson led over 1,000 slaves to freedom. Mason aided about 1,300 slaves on their journeys to the North. On one trip John Mason was captured and sold into slavery. He soon escaped and continued his work on the Underground Railroad.

Harriet Tubman traveled to the South nineteen times and freed more than three hundred slaves.

Slave owners hated the Abolitionists. These Abolitionists were a threat to slavery. The slave owners wrote books and articles against the anti-slavery groups. Their arguments were based on the racist ideas that all Negroes were inferior to all whites. They concluded that Negroes were like children and could not live properly as free men. The Negroes needed masters to take care of them. Many southern ministers said that slavery was good because it gave Negro slaves a chance to learn about the Christian religion. Planters said that the South could not grow its large cotton crop without the help of slaves. They said that the end of slavery would mean the ruin of the South. Who would grow the crops? Who would be able to find a source of labor as cheap as slave labor? What would happen to the status of the planters?

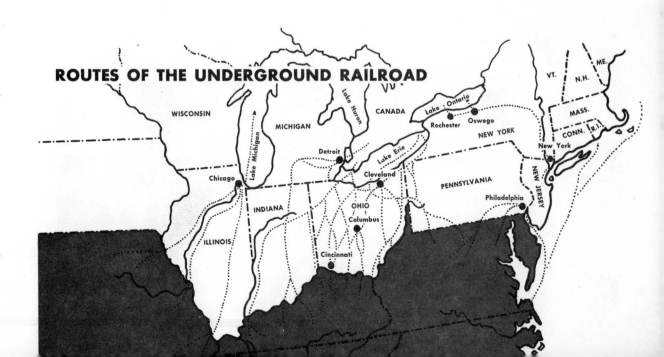

ROUTES OF THE UNDERGROUND RAILROAD

Finally, political leaders, such as John C. Calhoun, said that the Negro slaves were better off and happier than the free, white factory workers of the North. He argued that slaves were taken care of when they were sick or got old. No one looked after a factory worker who was sick or old. He pointed out that slaves always had clothes, food, and shelter. No slave was ever out of a job or went without food. Sometimes in the North a worker would be fired from his job. When this happened he went without food and was turned out of his house when he didn't pay the rent. Also, he said, many free workers in the North earned very little money and actually lived worse than many slaves lived.

The conflict between Abolitionists and the supporters of slavery helped cause the Civil War. This war lasted from 1861 to 1865. On January 1, 1863, President Abraham Lincoln proclaimed the freedom of all slaves living in the states that had rebelled against the federal government. This proclamation was called the *Emancipation Proclamation*. To help make this proclamation come true, over 186,000 Negro men fought in the Union Army. They took part in 198 battles and suffered 68,000 casualties. Sixteen Negro soldiers and five Negro sailors were awarded the *Congressional Medal of Honor*. This is the highest military award of the United States. It is given only for military acts of heroism.

The Underground Railroad used every possible means of transportation to help slaves escape from the South.

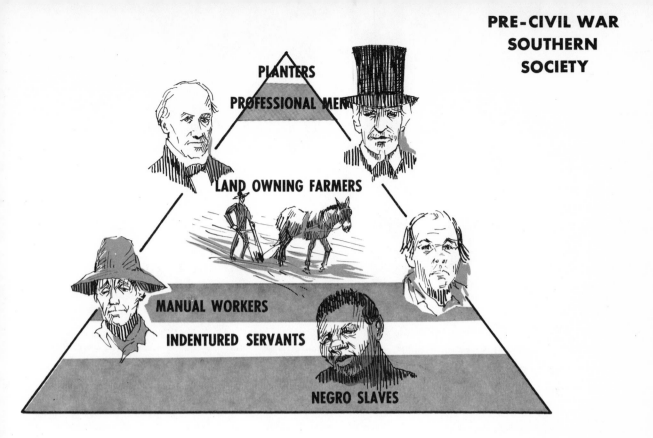

PLANTERS
PROFESSIONAL MEN
LAND OWNING FARMERS
MANUAL WORKERS
INDENTURED SERVANTS
NEGRO SLAVES

**How did slavery affect the progress
of American Negroes?**

Certainly slavery has made a lasting impression on the lives of all American Negroes. It has hindered their chances to make progress. It has affected the way white people think about Negroes. It has also affected the way many Negroes think about themselves.

People are always comparing themselves with the people living around them. They notice that some people have more education, better homes, more money, better jobs, and a more attractive way of life than they do. We usually give more respect, honor, and prestige to people who have these better things of life. We say these people have a higher *status* than other people who do not have these things. Some people earn a high status because they are smarter and work harder than other people. Education and hard work help an individual gain status. Their status is achieved. Other people enjoy a high status from the day they were born. It might be because they belong to an important family. Their status is given or ascribed. Another example of ascribed status is the special status given to older people. Children have a lower status than adults. There is nothing that can be done to change this status relationship between adults and children. It is a custom of our society. This custom has been handed down from generation to generation.

Planters often built large and beautiful houses. These houses showed the high status enjoyed by the planters. The low status slaves lived in shacks in the back of the plantation house.

From the day of their birth, Negro slaves had the lowest status of any Americans. They were thought to be inferior to all other people. They were given little or no respect. They were considered only as property not as human beings. The only way a slave could improve his status was to run away from his master and become a free man. But the status of a free Negro was not much higher than the status of a slave; most white Americans thought all Negroes were born inferior. Many Americans thought that all Negroes should be slaves. A low status was given to every Negro from the time of his birth.

There was nothing that could be done to improve this low ascribed status. It was an American tradition.

The poorest white man with little or no education had a higher status than any Negro. Even free Negroes with wealth, education, and intelligence were considered to have less status than the lowest white man. Because most Negroes in America were slaves, white Americans came to believe that Negroes were fit only to be slaves. The owners of the large plantations had the highest status of anyone in the South. His slaves had the lowest status. No individual could change this American tradition.

The low ascribed status of all Negroes did much to hinder their progress. Negroes were expected to behave differently than other people. Just as a child is expected to obey and respect his parents and teachers, Negroes were expected to obey and respect all white people. Negroes were expected to be obedient, meek, humble, happy, cowardly, carefree, stupid, and ambitionless. This was the *role* that went with the status of a Negro. Just as an actor in a play is expected to perform a certain role in a certain way, so Negroes were expected to play their special role whenever they were around white people. Whenever Negroes failed to play their expected role, most whites treated them badly. Slaves or free Negroes who refused to play their role were whipped or even killed.

Handbills, such as this, were passed out all over the South in an attempt to capture fugitive slaves.

"NOT SO FAST BOY—YOU'RE SUPPOSED TO JUST SHUFFLE ALONG."

The low status and role of American Negroes during the time of slavery made a strong imprint on the minds of all Americans. Because of their low status, Negroes were forced to play a second class role to all white Americans. This caused most white people to think Negroes were not capable of improving their status or changing their role in life. This caused most white people to think Negroes were born inferior and were not able to behave in any other way.

Many artists during the time of slavery painted pictures that showed Negroes as always being happy and dancing.

These white people did not understand that the inferior role of Negroes was forced on them by the white people of America. They did not understand that behavior is not caused by race. They did not understand that if given a chance many Negroes could achieve a higher status and learn to play a different role in life and society.

Many Negroes were *handicapped* or crippled by the roles they were forced to play. From the time they were small children, they were told they were inferior. They were told they were not as good as white children. They were not given a chance to become educated or to become leaders. Most children, therefore, both Negro and white, had learned by the time they were adults that Negroes were inferior to whites. Many Negroes, therefore, believed they really were inferior to whites. They believed they could never be as good as white people no matter how hard they tried. They did not try, therefore, to improve their status. They had been taught to believe that this was impossible. It was impossible for any Negro who believed these ideas to make any real progress in the way he lived, the role he played, or his status in life.

The handicaps of the slavery system continued to hurt the Negro people long after slavery was ended in America. Since most slaves could only work as servants or laborers, they had not learned how to become highly skilled workers. Very few slaves learned how to read or write. They were seldom given the opportunity to be responsible for their own lives. Living under these conditions as a slave did not allow people to be prepared to take care of themselves. When freedom suddenly came at the end of the Civil War in 1865, many of the newly freed Negroes were helpless and confused. They did not know what to do with their new freedom. They had been trained only to be slaves, and so were unprepared when they gained their freedom.

One of the jobs of the Freedmen's Bureau was to find employment for the ex-slaves.

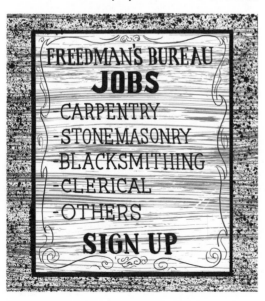

FREEDMAN'S BUREAU
JOBS
-CARPENTRY
-STONEMASONRY
-BLACKSMITHING
-CLERICAL
-OTHERS
SIGN UP

School Enrollment 1850 1950

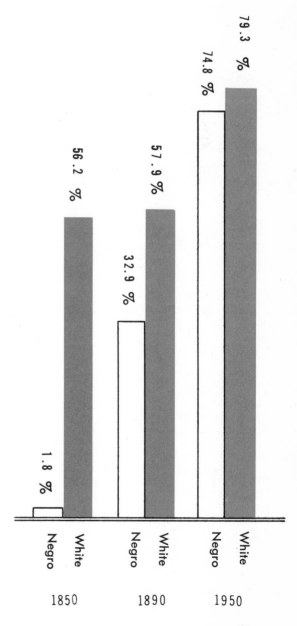

	1850		1890		1950
Negro	1.8 %	White 56.2 %	Negro 32.9 %	White 57.9 %	Negro 74.8 % White 79.3 %

LIFE OF A SLAVE IN MARYLAND

Frederick Douglass was born as a slave in Talbot County, Maryland. In 1838, at age twenty-one, he escaped from slavery and went to live in New York City. Soon he became a leader in the anti-slavery movement. He described his life as a slave in *Narrative of the Life of Frederick Douglass: An American Slave*. This book was published in Boston by the American Anti-Slavery Society in 1845.

The plantation is about twelve miles north of Easton, in Talbot country, and is situated on the border of Miles River. The principal products raised upon it were tobacco, corn, and wheat. . . .

Colonel Lloyd kept from three to four hundred slaves on his home plantation, and owned a large number more on the neighboring farms belonging to him. . . .

The men and women slaves received, as their monthly allowance of food, eight pounds of pork, or its equivalent in fish, and one bushel of corn meal. Their yearly clothing consisted of two coarse linen shirts, one pair of linen trousers for winter, made of coarse negro cloth, one pair of stockings, and one pair of shoes, the whole of which could not have cost more than seven dollars. The allowance of the slave children was given to their mothers, or to the old women taking care of them. The children unable to work in the field had neither shoes, stockings, jackets, nor trousers, given to them; their clothing consisted of two coarse linen shirts per year. . . .

There were no beds given the slaves, unless one coarse blanket be considered such, and none but the men and women had these. . . . They find less difficulty from the want of beds, than from the want of time to sleep; for when their day's work in the field is done, the most of them have their washing, mending, and cooking to do, and having few or none of the ordinary facilities for doing either of these, very many of their sleeping hours are consumed in preparing for the field the coming day; and when this is done, old and young, male and female, married and single, drop down side by side, on one common bed, — the cold, damp floor, — each covering himself or herself with their miserable blankets; and here they sleep till they are summoned to the field by the driver's horn. . . . Mr. Severe, the overseer, used to stand by the door of the quarter, armed with a large hickory stick and heavy cowskin, ready to whip any one who was so unfortunate as not to hear, or, from any other cause, was prevented from being ready to start for the field at the sound of the horn. . . .

I was probably between seven and eight years old when I left Colonel Lloyd's plantation. I left it with joy. My old master . . . had determined to let me go to Baltimore to live with Mr. Hugh Auld. . . .

Very soon after I went to live with Mr. and Mrs. Auld, she was very kindly commenced to teach me the A,B,C. After I had learned this, she assisted me in learning to spell words of three or four letters. Just at this point of my progress, Mr. Auld found out what was going on, and at once forbade Mrs. Auld to instruct me further, telling her, among other things, that it was unlawful, as well as unsafe, to teach a slave to read. To use his own words, further, he said, "If you give a nigger an inch, he will take an ell. A nigger should know nothing but to obey his master—to do as he is told to do. Learning would spoil the best nigger in the world. Now if you teach that nigger (speaking of me) how to read, there would be no keeping him. It would forever unfit him to be a slave. He would at once become unmanageable, and of no value to his master. As to himself, it would do him no good, but a great deal of harm. It would make him discontented and unhappy." These words sank deep into my heart. . . . I now understood . . . the white man's power to enslave the black man. . . . From that moment I understood the pathway from slavery to freedom. . . .

. . . Master Hugh hired me to Mr. William Gardner, an extensive ship-builder, on Fell's Point. . . . In entering the shipyard, my orders from Mr. Gardner were to do whatever the carpenters commanded me to do. This was placing me at the beck and call of about seventy-five men. I was to regard all these as masters. Their word was to be my law. My situation was a most trying one. At times I needed a dozen pair of hands. I was called a dozen ways in the space of a single minute. Three or four voices would strike my ear at the same moment. It was—"Fred, come help me to cant this timber here."—"Fred, come carry this timber yonder."—"Fred, bring that roller here."—"Fred, go get a fresh can of water.'—"Fred, come help saw off the end of this timber."—"Fred, go quick and get the crowbar . . ."—"Halloo, nigger! come, turn this grindstone. . . ."

This was my school for eight months; and I might have remained there longer, but for a most horrid fight I had with four of the white apprentices, in which my left eye was nearly knocked out, and I was horribly mangled in other respects. The facts in the case were these: Until a very little while after I went there, white and black ship-carpenters worked side by side. . . . All hands seemed to be well satisfied. Many of the black carpenters were freemen. Things seemed to be going on very well. All at once, the white carpenters knocked off, and said they would not work with free colored workmen. Their reason for this, as alleged, was, that if free colored carpenters were encouraged, they would soon take the trade into their own hands, and poor white men would be thrown out of employment. They therefore felt called upon at once to put a stop to it. And . . . they broke off, swearing they would work no longer, unless he would discharge his black carpenters. Now, though this did not extend to me in form, it did reach me in fact. My fellow-apprentices very soon began to feel it degrading to them to work with me. They began to put on airs, and talk about the "nigger" taking the country, saying we all ought to be killed; and, being encouraged by the journey-men, they commenced making my condition as hard as they could, by hectoring me around, and sometimes striking me. I . . . struck back . . . and while I kept them from combining, I succeeded very well; for I could whip the whole of them, taking them separately. They, however, at length combined, and came upon me, armed with sticks, stones, and heavy handspikes. One came in front with a half brick. There was one at each side of me, and one behind me .While I was attending to those in front, and on either side, the one behind ran up with the handspike, and struck me a heavy blow upon the head. It stunned me. I fell, and with this they all ran upon me, and fell to beating me with their fists. I let them lay on for a while, gathering strength. In an instant, I gave a sudden surge, and rose to my hands and knees. Just as I did that, one of their number, with his heavy boot, gave me a powerful kick in the left eye. My eyeball seemed to have burst. When they saw my eye closed, and badly swollen, they left me. With this I seized the handspike, and for a time pursued them. But here the carpenters interfered, and I thought I might as well give it up. It was impossible to stand my hand against so many. All this took place in sight of not less than fifty white ship-carpenters, and not one interposed a friendly word; but some cried, "Kill the damned nigger! Kill him! Kill him! He struck a white person." I found my only chance for life was in flight. I succeeded in getting away without an additional blow, and barely so; for to strike a white man is death by Lynch Law, — and that was the law in Mr. Gardner's ship-yard. . . .

SLAVERY ON A COTTON PLANTATION IN LOUISIANA

Soloman Northrup was born free and lived in New York. In 1841 he was kidnapped by slave traders while visiting Washington, D.C. He was shipped to a slave market in New Orleans. There he was sold to a cotton planter and was sent to work as a slave along the Boeuf River in Louisiana. He escaped from slavery and wrote about his experiences in *Twelve Years a Slave*. This book was published in 1853.

In the latter part of August begins the cotton-picking season. At this time each slave is presented with a sack. A strap is fastened to it, which goes over the neck, holding the mouth of the sack breast high, while the bottom reaches nearly to the ground. Each one is also presented with a large basket that will hold about two barrels. This is to put the cotton into when the sack is filled. The baskets are carried to the field and placed at the beginning of the rows. . . .

An ordinary day's work is two hundred pounds. A slave who is accustomed to picking is punished if he or she brings in less quantity than that. . . .

The hands are required to be in the cotton field as soon as it is light in the morning. . . . With the exception of ten or fifteen minutes, which is given them at noon to swallow their allowance of cold bacon, they are not permitted to be a moment idle until it is too dark to see, and when the moon is full, they oftentimes labor till the middle of the night. They do not dare to stop even at dinner time, nor return to the quarters, however late it be, until the order to halt is given by the driver. The day's work over in the field, the baskets are "toted," or in other words, carried to the gin-house where the cotton is weighed. No matter how fatigued and weary he may be—no matter how much he longs for sleep and rest—a slave never approaches the gin-house with his basket of cotton but with fear. If it falls short in weight—if he has not performed the full task appointed him—he knows that he must suffer. . . .

This done, the labor of the day is not yet ended by any means. Each one must then attend to his respective chores. One feeds the mules, another the swine; another cuts wood, and so forth. Besides, the packing is all done by candlelight. Finally, at a late hour, they reach the slave quarters, sleepy and overcome by the long day's toil. Then a fire must be kindled in the cabin, the corn ground in the small hand mill, and supper and dinner for the next day prepared. . . .

The softest couches in the world are not to be found in the log mansion of the slave. The one whereon I reclined year after year was a plank twelve inches wide and ten feet long. My pillow was a stick of wood. The bedding was a coarse blanket, and not a rag or shred besides. Moss might be used, were it not that it directly breeds a swarm of fleas.

The cabin is constructed of logs, without floor or window. The latter is altogether unnecessary, the crevices between the logs admitting sufficient light. In stormy weather the rain drives through them, rendering it comfortless and extremely disagreeable. The rude door hangs on great wooden hinges. In one end is constructed an awkward fireplace.

An hour before daylight the horn is blown. Then the slaves arise, prepare their breakfast, fill a gourd with water, in another deposit their dinner of cold bacon and corn cake, and hurry to the field again. It is an offence . . . followed by a flogging to be found at the slave quaters after daybreak. Then the fears and labors of another day begin, and until its close, there is no such thing as rest. The slave fears he will be caught lagging through the day; he fears to approach the gin-house with his basketload of cotton at night; he fears when he lies down that he will oversleep in the morning.

A DEFENSE OF SLAVERY

George Fitzhugh was a leading defender of the institution of slavery. He was born in 1806 in Prince Williams County, Virginia. Later his family owned a five hundred acre plantation in King George County, Virginia. Fitzhugh was a lawyer, but he spent most of his time speaking and writing in support of slavery.

Now it is clear . . . democracy would not suit a negro nation, nor will the government of law suffice for the individual negro. He is but a grown up child, and must be governed as a child. . . . The master occupies towards him the place of parent or guardian. . . .

. . . the negro race is inferior to the white race, and living in their midst, they would be far outstripped or outwitted in the chase of free competition. Gradual but certain extermination would be their fate. . . .

We would remind those who . . . sympathize with negro slavery, that his slavery here relieves him from a far more cruel slavery in Africa . . . and every brutal vice and crime that can disgrace humanity; and that it christianizes, protects, supports and civilizes him; that it governs him far better than free laborers at the North are governed. . . . Our negroes are not only better off as to physical comfort than free laborers, but their moral condition is better. . . .

Would the abolitionists approve of a system of society that set white children free . . . to all the rights, both as to person and property, which belong to adults? Would it be criminal or praiseworthy to do so? Criminal, of course. Now, are the average negroes equal in formation, in native intelligence . . . to well informed white children of fourteen? We who have lived with them for forty years, think not. The competition of the world would be too much for the children. They would be cheated out of their property and debased in their morals. Yet they would meet everywhere with sympathizing friends of their own color, ready to aid, advise and assist them. The negro would be exposed to the same competition and greater temptations, with no greater ability to contend with them, and with these additional difficulties. He would be welcome nowhere; meet with thousands of enemies and no friends. If he went North, the white laborers would kick him and cuff him, and drive him out of employment. . . .

Look closely into slavery, and you will see nothing so hideous in it. . . .

The Southerner is the negro's friend, his only friend. Let no . . . abolitionist . . . dissolve this friendship.

The negro slaves of the South are the happiest, and, in some sense, the freest people in the world. The children and the aged and infirm work not at all, and yet have all the comforts and necessaries of life provided for them. They enjoy liberty, because they are oppressed neither by care nor labor. The women do little hard work, and are protected . . . by their masters. The negro men and stout boys work, on the average, in good weather, not more than nine hours a day. The balance of their time is spent in perfect abandon. Besides they have their Sabbaths and holidays. . . . With their faces upturned to the sun, they can sleep at any hour; and quiet sleep is the greatest of human enjoyments. . . . We no not know whether free laborers ever sleep. . . . The free laborer must work or starve. He is more of a slave than the negro, because he works longer and harder for less allowance than the slave, and has no holiday, because the cares of life with him begin when its labors end. He has no liberty, and not a single right. . . .

Free laborers have not a thousandth part of the rights and liberties of negro slaves. Indeed, they have not a single right or a single liberty, unless it be the right or liberty to die.

SLAVERY ON A VIRGINIA PLANTATION

Frederick Law Olmstead was a white newspaper writer from New York. He traveled through the southern states to observe the slavery system. He later wrote several books about slavery. This document was taken from *A Journey in the Seaboard Slave States* in 1856.

After breakfast has been eaten early in the cabins, at sunrise or a little before in winter, and perhaps a little later in summer, they go to the fields. At noon dinner is brought to them, and, unless the work presses, they are allowed two hours' rest. Very punctually at sunset they stop work and are at liberty. . . . Thus they work in the field about eleven hours a day on an average. Returning to their cabins . . . they then make a fire . . . and cook their own supper, which will be a bit of bacon fried, often with eggs, corn-bread . . . and perhaps some sweet potatoes roasted in the ashes. Immediately after supper they go to sleep, often lying on the floor or a bench. . . .

The houses of the slaves are usually logcabins, of various degrees of comfort. . . . At one end there is a great open fireplace, which is exterior to the wall of the house, being made of clay in an inclosure, about eight feet square and high, of logs. The chimney is sometimes of brick, but more commonly of lath or split sticks, laid up like log-work and plastered with mud.

As to the clothing of slaves on the plantations, they are said to be usually furnished by their owners or masters, every year, each with a coat and trousers . . . , two pairs of strong shoes, or one pair of strong boots and one of lighter shoes for harvest; three shirts; one blanket; and one felt hat.

The women have two dresses of striped cotton, three shifts, two pairs of shoes. . . . On Sundays and holidays they usually look very smart, but when at work, very ragged and slovenly.

Using Historical Methods

1. List everything in this chapter that can be considered a document. Why is each thing on your list a document?

2. Which documents are primary and which are secondary sources?

3. What opinions are contained in the quotation by Emerson?

4. What conclusions can be formed from the graph on page thirty-six?

5. What conclusions can be formed from the graph on page fifty-one?

6. What conclusions can be formed from the stories of the revolts of Prosser, Deslondes, Vessey, and Turner?

7. What facts and opinions are stated by Frederick Douglass?

8. What conclusions are formed by Douglass? What conclusions do you form after reading this document written by Douglass?

9. What facts and opinions are stated by George Fitzhugh?

10. What conclusions are formed by George Fitzhugh?

11. What are the differences in the conclusions of Fitzhugh and Douglass?

12. What new questions are raised by each of the documents in this chapter?

Knowing Your Vocabulary

slavery /ˈslāv-(ə)-rē/
When a group of people have no freedom and are under the control of other people. 31

indentured servant /in-ˈden-chərd ˈsər-vənt/
People who lose their freedom for a certain number of years in order to repay a debt. They were set free after this period of time. 32

Middle Passage /ˈmid-əl ˈpas-ij/
The name given to the crossing of the Atlantic Ocean by the ships carrying slaves to the New World. 35

planter /ˈplant-ər/
Rich farm owner in the South before the Civil War. 36

cotton gin /ˈkät-ən-ˈjin/
A machine invented by Eli Whitney to separate the seeds from the cotton fiber. 36

house slave /ˈhau̇s-ˈslāv/
Slaves that were housekeepers, cooks, and workers in the house of the plantation. 38

field slave /ˈfē(ə)ld ˈslāv/
Slaves that did the heavy farm work on the plantations. 38

overseer /ˈō-və(r)-ˌsi(ə)r/
A man hired to be the boss of a group of slave workers. 38

rebellion /ri-ˈbel-yən/
A violent uprising to overthrow the power of the people who are presently ruling. 39

militia /mə-ˈlish-ə/
A local or state army, usually called during public emergencies. 41

Abolition Movement /ˌab-ə-ˈlish-ən ˈmüv-mənt/
A group of people who joined together to end slavery in the United States. 42

Underground Railroad /ˈən-dər-ˌgrau̇nd ˈrā(ə)l-ˌrōd/
The many escape routes that were used by slaves fleeing the South. 43

Emancipation Proclamation
/i-ˌman(t)-sə-ˈpā-shən-ˌpräk-lə-ˈmā-shən/
A document issued by President Lincoln that freed all slaves living in the states rebelling against the federal government. 46

Congressional Medal of Honor
/ˈkäŋ-grəs-shən-əl-ˈmed-əl- əv-ˈän-ər/
The highest military award given by
the United States. 46

status /ˈstāt-əs/
Status is the rank or position that a
person holds among the people with
whom he lives. 47

role /ˈrōl/
The actions that a person is expected
to perform. 49

handicapped /ˈhan-di-ˌkap-(ə)d/
Not to have the equal chances for
success that are given to other people. 50

Reading the Text

1. Among what people of the world
has slavery existed?

2. Why did the United States outlaw slavery?

3. What is the difference between
an indentured servant and a
slave?

4. Why were not the Indians en-
slaved like the Negroes?

5. Why was the invention of the
cotton gin important for the plantation owners?

6. What were some of the worst features of life as a slave on a plantation?

7. What are some of the arguments
used by the planters when they
stated that slavery was good for
the Negro?

8. Who are some of the people who
had high status in the South before the Civil War?

9. What was the role the Negro
had to play when he was around
white people? Why did he have
to play this role?

10. What was the status of a Negro
slave?

11. Why was is difficult if not impossible for a slave to improve his
status and role?

12. What evidence of racism can you
find in the documents in this
chapter?

13. How does racism help explain
some of the problems of American Negroes during the era of
slavery?

Identifying Names and Places

Frederick Douglass
Harriet Tubman
slavery system
Middle Passage
plantation system
Nat Turner
Denmark Vessey
Abolition Movement
The Liberator
Underground Railroad
Levi Coffin
John Mason
Emancipation Proclamation

Debating and Discussing Ideas

1. Arrange a class debate. Have one group be planters who want slavery continued. Have the other group be members of the Abolition Movement.

2. Have a class discussion about the causes of slavery. Why was it practiced in the United States?

3. Have a class discussion on the effects of slavery. What effects has slavery had on white Americans? What effects has slavery had on Negro Americans?

Reading Other Sources

Ansley, Delight, *The Sword and the Spirit*, New York: Crowell, 1955.

Bontemps, Arna, *Frederick Douglass: Slave — Fighter — Freeman*, New York: Knopf, 1959.

Buckmaster, Henrietta, *Flight to Freedom: The Story of the Underground Railroad*, New York: Crowell, 1958.

Buckmaster, Henrietta, *Let My People Go*, Boston: Beacon, 1959.

Fuller, Edmund, *A Star Pointed North*, New York: Harper and Row, 1946.

Graham, Shirley, *There Was Once A Slave*, New York: Messner, 1947.

Meadowcroft, Enid LaMonte, *By Secret Railway*, New York: Crowell, 1948.

Nolan, Jeanette Covert, *John Brown*, New York: Messner, 1950.

Sterling, Dorothy, *Forever Free, the Story of the Emancipation Proclamation*, Garden City, New York: Doubleday, 1963.

3. Reconstruction

*The most certain test by which we judge
whether a country is really free
is the amount of security enjoyed by minorities.*

Lord Acton
The History of Freedom in Antiquity

What was Reconstruction?

How does a war-divided country once again become a united nation? How do people who have faced each other with hatred on the battlefield once again become friends? How can people who have been slaves get along in peace and friendship with the people who have been their masters? How can people who have been slaves learn to take care of themselves once they are free? These were some of the main problems faced by the United States after the Civil War.

Reconstruction is the name given to the twelve years following the Civil War. From 1865 until 1877, the federal government tried to bind the nation together again. The federal government tried to solve some of these problems. The federal gorvenment tried to change the status and the role of Negroes by passing laws to help the Negro people. These laws were meant to give Negroes the same rights as other Americans. These laws were meant to change or reconstruct the way of life in the South. These laws led to many conflicts between the federal govenrment and the governments of the southern states. These laws also led to some conflicts between southern whites and Negroes. These conflicts arose because many southern whites did not want to reconstruct their way of life. Many southerners believed they were right and that the North was wrong. They would not change.

How was Reconstruction carried out?

The first steps of Reconstruction came even before the Civil War had ended. Many people in the South badly needed help. The South had suffered greatly during the war. Plantations, farms, roads, and towns were in ruins. The government of the southern states had broken down when the Union Army invaded the South. For awhile there were no laws, no policemen, no courts, and no officials to stop people from stealing, murdering, and destroying property. Homeless and hungry people wandered around the countryside. Former slaves were frightened and confused. They had no jobs, no food, no money, no homes, and no friends. The federal government appointed military commanders to try and solve these problems. An army commander was appointed for each state as soon as that state surrendered to the Union Army. A *Freedman's Bureau* was set up in March, 1865, to provide Negroes with food, clothing, medical care, education, and protection from violence and terror.

The Freedman's Bureau was a strong force in helping Negroes become accustomed to their newly gained freedom. The Freedman's Bureau transported homeless people to new areas where they might find jobs, new homes, new friends, and a new way of life. The Freedman's Bureau tried to solve the problems of two hundred years of slavery.

By 1867 the Bureau operated forty-six hospitals for former slaves. In these hospitals of the Freedman's Bureau, doctors tried to improve the health of the former slaves. Over $2 million was spent treating 450,000 cases of sickness and disease.

The Bureau also tried to protect Negroes from being cheated out of their wages and property. Investigators were sent all over the South to see that the property rights of Negroes were protected.

The Freedman's Bureau probably achieved its greatest success in the field of education. It established elementary schools, high schools, colleges, and universities. By 1870, $5 million had been spent on education for the former slaves, and there were 247,333 Negro pupils in 4,329 schools in the South.

The next step in Reconstruction came on December 18, 1865, when the Thirteenth Amendment was added to the United States Constitution. This *amendment*, addition to the Constitution, outlawed slavery in the United States. Two years earlier, President Lincoln had issued the Emancipation Proclamation. This proclamation gave freedom to all slaves living in the Confederate states. But the slave states of Missouri, Kentucky, Delaware, and Maryland had remained with the Union during the Civil War. At the end of the Civil War, many southerners hoped that Negroes would once again be made slaves. But the Thirteenth Amendment ended slavery everywhere and forever in the United States.

The Freedman's Bureau built housing and operated schools for the ex-slaves.

62

What were the different Reconstruction plans?

There were many different plans for Reconstruction after the Civil War. Many arguments broke out among the supporters of the different Reconstruction plans. Before the end of the Civil War, President Lincoln had formed his plan of Reconstruction for the South. Lincoln wanted to be lenient with the South. He had a plan that made it easy for the southern states to set-up new governments and again join the Union. Also, Lincoln offered *pardons* —release from the penalty of jail or fine—to all except a few high Confederate leaders and officials.

Following Lincoln's plan, some southern states began to form new governments right after the end of the war. But some members of Congress thought that Lincoln's plan was too lenient. These members of Congress thought that Reconstruction should be handled by Congress and not by the President. These members of Congress feared that the same people would remain in power in the South if Lincoln's plan was used. They feared that Negroes would not be given equal rights. These Congressmen were called Radical Republicans. Thaddeus Stevens in the House of Representatives and Charles Sumner in the Senate were two of the leading Radical Republicans who fought for the right of Congress to plan Reconstruction.

Charles Sumner (top) from Massachusetts and Thaddeus Stevens (bottom) from Pennsylvania were two of the leading Radical Republicans.

President Lincoln was *assassinated* in April, 1865; Lincoln was murdered by John Wilkes Booth. Andrew Johnson became the new President of the United States. Johnson was a southerner and a former slave owner. He declared, however, that he would follow Lincoln's plan of Reconstruction. The Republicans in Congress thought that Johnson was a racist and wanted to return the Negro to slavery. The dispute between Johnson and the Republicans in Congress was won by the Congress. Congress passed its own Reconstruction Act over the *veto* or objection of President Johnson.

The Reconstruction Act said the former Confederate states were to be divided into five military districts. Each military district was to be ruled by an army commander and his men. Tennessee was left out of this plan because Tennessee had been readmitted to the Union in 1866. The purpose of the military rule was to prepare the former Confederate states for readmittance into the Union. The Union soldiers were to rule these states until the states were able to form new governments for themselves. All Negro and white people who could prove they were loyal to the United States were told to elect representatives to a state convention. Anyone who had been a rebel against the United States could not vote or take part in these conventions. These state conventions were to write a new constitution for each of the southern states. All of these states were readmitted to the Union by 1870 and were sending representatives to Congress. Only people who could prove they were loyal to the United States were allowed to vote or to hold office.

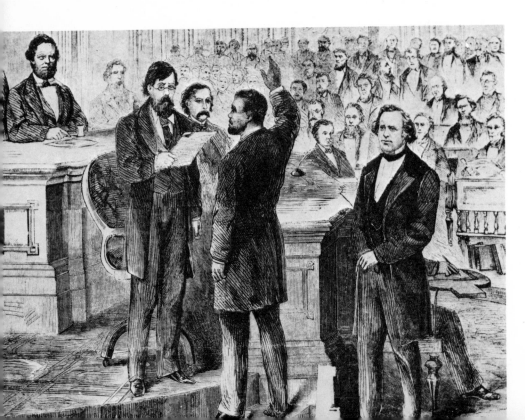

Hiram Revels takes his oath of office as a United States Senator. Revels was one of two Negroes elected to the Senate during Reconstruction.

During Reconstruction, Negroes were often pictured as being lazy, happy, dancing, or sleeping. Such illustrations helped form white opinions about Negroes.

The only people who could vote, therefore, were the Negroes, northerners who came to the South, and a few southerners who cooperated with the Union Army. The northerners who came south were called *carpetbaggers*. Southerners who cooperated with carpetbaggers, Union troops, or federal officials were called *scalawags*. Former Confederate government officials and army officers were denied the right to take part in the new southern state governments.

Negroes played an important role in all of these state governments. They had the greatest influence in South Carolina. From 1865 until 1874, more Negroes than whites were elected to public office. Only one Negro, P.B.S. Pinchback of Louisiana, served as a state governor. Pinchback had been elected lieutenant-governor of Louisiana. In 1873 the elected governor was removed from office and Pinchback served as governor for forty-three days.

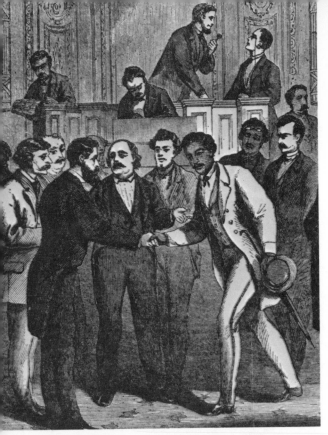

John W. Menard was the first Negro representative to be elected to the United States Congress.

Blanche K. Bruce was one of two Negro senators elected during Reconstruction.

Perhaps the most outstanding Negroes who served as public officials during Reconstruction were Robert B. Elliott and Francis L. Cardozo. Both were from South Carolina. Elliott was speaker of the South Carolina House of Representatives in 1874. Cardozo was the South Carolina Secretary of State from 1868 to 1872, and he then served as State Treasurer from 1872 to 1876.

Many Negroes also served in the United States Congress. Between 1867 and 1901, two Negroes served in the Senate, and twenty Negroes served in the House of Representatives. Hiram R. Revels and Blanche K. Bruce of Mississippi were the two United States Senators.

One of the most important things the Reconstruction governments did was to establish a public school system in the South. This meant that all children would have a chance to go to school. Before the Civil War, only children from wealthy families had the chance to go to school. Most of the children from wealthy families would attend a private school. There were no free, public school systems in any of the southern states before the Civil War. Very few of the poor white or Negro people had learned to read or to write. The Reconstruction governments of the southern states made it possible for both Negro and white people to send their children to free, public schools to get an education.

AMENDMENT XIII

SECTION 1. Neither slavery nor involuntary servitude, except as a punishment for crime whereof the party shall have been duly convicted, shall exist within the United States, or any place subject to their jurisdiction.

SECTION 2. Congress shall have power to enforce this article by appropriate legislation.

AMENDMENT XIV

SECTION 1. All persons born or naturalized in the United States, and subject to the jurisdiction thereof, are citizens of the United States and of the State wherein they reside. No State shall make or enforce any law which shall abridge the privileges or immunities of citizens of the United States; nor shall any State deprive any person of life, liberty, or property, without due process of law; nor deny to any person within its jurisdiction the equal protection of the laws.

SECTION 2. (Omitted)

SECTION 3. (Omitted)

SECTION 4. (Omitted)

SECTION 5. (Omitted)

AMENDMENT XV

SECTION 1. The right of citizens of the United States to vote shall not be denied or abridged by the United States or any State on account of race, color, or previous condition of servitude.

SECTION 2. The Congress shall have power to enforce this article by appropriate legislation.

The Reconstruction governments also passed many other reform laws. These laws were aimed at giving equal rights and opportunities to all people in the South. All adult males were given the right to vote and to hold office in every southern state. Previously some of the states had allowed only property owners to vote or to hold public office in the state government.

The federal government made some other important laws during the Reconstruction period. On July 28, 1868, the Fourteenth Amendment became part of the Constitution of the United States. This amendment said all Negroes were citizens of the United States. It also said no state government could take away the rights or privileges of any citizen.

One such right guaranteed by the Fourteenth Amendment was that all citizens must receive equal protection under the law. This means there can not be one law for white people and another law for Negro people.

The Fifteenth Amendment was added to the Constitution on March 30, 1870. This amendment said no state government could take away the right to vote from any of its citizens. This amendment was meant to protect the voting rights of Negroes in America.

Congress also passed a Civil Rights Act on March 1, 1875. This law said that is was not legal to withold equal service from Negroes in hotels, restaurants, trains, theaters, or any other public facility in any of the states of the United States.

forty acres and a mule

One suggestion to help the freedmen was to give every family forty acres and a mule. This suggestion was never taken seriously.

How did Reconstruction affect the progress of American Negroes?

Reconstruction seemed like a time of great progress for the Negro people. It seemed that the status of many Negroes was rising. Some Negroes were taking leadership roles in the government. Many Negroes were going to school to prepare themselves for better jobs and a better way of life and a different role in life.

But there was another side to Reconstruction. Most Negroes were unable to go to school. This meant that the only jobs they could find were difficult laboring jobs. Farming was the job that most Negroes had done

while they were slaves. Now, very few Negroes were able to become landowners. Congressman Thaddeus Stevens from Pennsylvania once said that every freedman should be given "forty acres and a mule." This plan was never taken seriously by the lawmakers. As a result, many Negroes wandered around the country without jobs and without a permanent home. Others went back to work for the large plantation owners. Some Negroes even stayed on the same plantation where they had been slaves just a few years earlier. They were not much better off than in the days when they were slaves. Wages for Negro plantation workers were from $5 to $15 a month. They also were given food and shelter.

Most Negroes became *sharecroppers*. This meant they farmed a small plot of land owned by someone else. In return for the privilege of working this land, the sharecropper had to give a part of his crop to the landowner. In some cases the sharecropper had to give 70 or 80 percent of his crops to the landowner. Thus, the landowner made a profit from the work of the sharecropper. The landowner also made a profit when he sold cloth, seeds, and other goods to the sharecropper. The sharecropper was usually in debt to the landowner. This system of sharecropping almost always meant the Negro would live in poverty. It was little better than slavery.

The Freedman's Bureau. which had been so helpful to many Negroes, was shut down in 1872. Some white people complained that the Bureau was wasting money foolishly by trying to help Negroes. Others said it was unfair to white people for Negroes to keep getting free services from the Freedman's Bureau. Congress listened to these arguments and closed the Freedman's Bureau.

Why was Reconstruction a failure?

The most important reason for the failure of Reconstruction was that many white people both northerners and southerners did not agree with the changes Reconstruction would have made. Reconstruction did not bring full equality or freedom to the Negroes because most white people did not want Negroes to have these rights. They believed Negroes were fit only to be slaves or laborers or servants. It disturbed these white people to see Negroes voting, holding public offices, and mixing socially with white people. Most of all it disturbed these white people to see former slaves rising to positions of importance and superiority over white people.

Southerners did not like it that Reconstruction plans were made by the federal government in Washington, D.C. and were enforced by federal soldiers in the South. Many southerners did not like to be told what to do and ordered around by people who were not from the South.

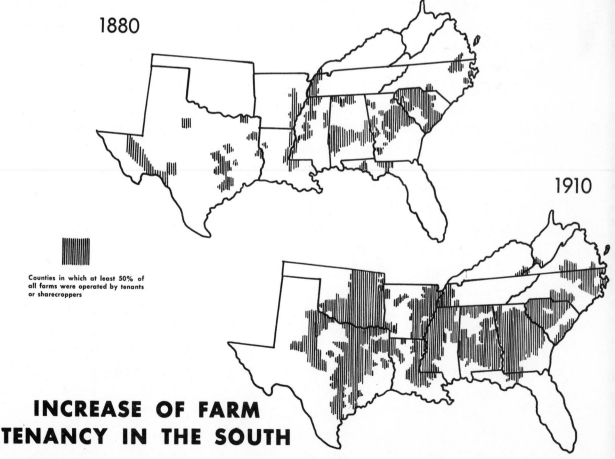

1880

1910

Counties in which at least 50% of
all farms were operated by tenants
or sharecroppers

INCREASE OF FARM
TENANCY IN THE SOUTH

The Ku Klux Klan prepares to execute a Republican. Republicans, carpetbaggers, scalawags, and Negroes were all targets of KKK violence.

How did the South resist the Reconstruction laws?

Many white people in the South decided to oppose Reconstruction in every possible way. Many secret organizations were formed to use terror and violence against the Negroes and against the whites who supported the Negro cause for equal rights. The most powerful of the organizations were the Knights of the White Camelia and the Knights of the Ku Klux Klan. Disguised in long, white, hooded garments, members of these organizations attempted to terrorize Negroes. They armed themselves with guns and swords and patrolled the countryside. Their purpose was to keep Negroes from making progress. They took the law into their own hands to achieve this purpose.

They threatened Negroes in order to keep them from voting. When Negroes refused to be scared by their threats, they would burn Negro businesses, homes, farms, and churches. Negroes were whipped, beaten, and even run out of their homes. Even murder was used to keep Negroes from participating in the election of public officials.

The federal government passed a Ku Klux Klan Act in 1871. This law was meant to protect Negroes from the terror of the Ku Klux Klan. The law, however, was not enforced. The Ku Klux Klan and other secret organizations were left to do their violent work. The cause of Negro equality and progress in the United States was damaged very seriously by this resistance to Reconstruction.

In 1872 former Confederate soldiers and government officials were given back their right to vote and to hold public office. The Ku Klux Klan had done its work well and had scared many Negroes away from voting. As a result the state governments of the South began to fall back into the hands of the same people as before the Civil War. These were the same people who had fought against the federal government in the Civil War. By 1875 the state governments of Virginia, North Carolina, Georgia, Texas, Arkansas, and Alabama had passed into the control of the southern Democrats. Only Louisiana, South Carolina, Florida, and Mississippi still had governments that supported the Reconstruction laws and Negro civil rights. The Ku Klux Klan and other similar groups were strong in all of these states that still supported Reconstruction. Each of these states was on the edge of armed conflict. The Ku Klux Klan and other white racist groups threatened to overthrow the governments of these remaining states.

When did Reconstruction end?

Reconstruction officially came to an end in 1877. The forces of white racism and white supremacy were allowed to take control of all of the states of the South. President Hayes withdrew the last federal troops from the South. He announced that the southern states were now able to take care of themselves without federal interference or control.

The problems resulting from the Civil War were not solved. The South was again united with the rest of the United States, but the South resented the federal government and refused to obey some of the federal laws. Hatred for northern Yankees and for Negroes remained strong in the South. And the Negroes of the South were left unprotected against the control of the white racists.

The Ku Klux Klan has remained strong in many areas of the United States. Here, a group of Klansmen march through the streets of Washington, D.C.

A NEGRO'S OPINION OF RECONSTRUCTION

On August 1, 1880, before a large gathering of Negro people, Frederick Douglass spoke of his disappointment with Reconstruction. He felt that the United States government had forgotten about helping the Negro people overcome the problems stemming from over two centuries of slavery. By this time Douglass had become the most important Negro civil rights leader.

How stands the case with the recently-emancipated millions of colored people in our own country? What is their condition today?

. . . today, in most of the Southern States, the fourteenth and fifteenth amendments are virtually nullified.

The rights which they were intended to guarantee are denied and held in contempt, The citizenship granted in the fourteenth amendment is practically a mockery, and the right to vote, provided for in the fifteenth amendment, is literally stamped out in fact of government. The old master class is today triumphant, and the newly-enfranchised class in a condition but little above that in which they were found before the rebellion.

Do you ask me how, after all that has been done, this state of things has been made possible? I will tell you. Our reconstruction measures were radically defective. They left the former slave completely in the power of old master, the loyal citizen in the hands of the disloyal rebel against the government. . . .

The old master class was not deprived of the power of life and death, which was the soul of the relation of master and slave. They could not, of course, sell their former slaves, but they retained the power to starve them to death, and wherever this power is held there is the power of slavery. He who can say to his fellow-man, "You shall serve me or starve," is a master and his subject is a slave. . . . Though no longer a slave, he is . . . compelled to work for whatever his employer is pleased to pay him, swindled out of his hard earnings by money orders redeemed in stores, compelled to pay the price of an acre of ground for its use during a single year, to pay more than four times more than a fair price for a pound of bacon and to be kept on the narrowest margin between life and starvation. Much complaint has been made that the freedmen have shown so little ability to take care of themselves since their emancipation. Men have marvelled that they have made so little progress. . . . To me the wonder is, not that the freedmen have made so little progress, but, rather, that they have made so much; not that they have been standing still, but that they have been able to stand at all.

We have only to reflect for a moment upon the situation in which these people found themselves when liberated. Consider their ignorance, their poverty, their destitution, and their absolute dependence upon the very class by which they had been held in bondage for centuries, a class whose every sentiment was averse to their freedom, and we shall be prepared to marvel that they have, under the circumtances, done so well. . . .

The very manner of their emancipation invited to the heads of the freedmen the bitterest hostility of race and class. They were hated because they had been slaves, hated because they were now free, and hated because of those who had freed them. . . .

When the serfs of Russia were emancipated, they were given three acres of ground upon which they could live and make a living. But not so when our slaves were emancipated. They were sent away empty-handed, without money, without friends, and without a foot of land upon which to stand. Old and young, sick and well, were turned loose to the open sky, naked to their enemies. The old slave quarter that had before sheltered them and the fields that had yielded them corn were now denied them. The old master class, in its wrath, said, "Clear out! The Yankees have freed you, now let them feed and shelter you!"

THE FREEDOM OF A FREEDMAN

Often the life of a freedman was little better than the life of a slave. In this document William Ward, a former slave, tells about his life during Reconstruction. This description is taken from *Lay My Burden Down: A Folk History of Slavery* which was published in 1945.

After the war was over, Old Man Gordon took me and some of the others out to Mississippi. I stayed in peonage out there for 'bout forty years. I was located at just 'bout forty miles south of Greenwood and I worked on the plantation of Old Man Sara Jones and Old Man Gordon.

I couldn't git away 'cause they watched us with guns all the time. When the levee busted, that kinda freed me. Man they was devils; they wouldn't 'low you to go nowhere—not even to church. You done good to get something to eat. They wouldn't give you no clothes, and if you got wet you just had to lay down in what you got wet in.

And man, they would whup you in spite of the devil. You had to ask to git water—if you didn't they would stretch you 'cross a barrel and wear you out. If you didn't work in a hurry, they would whup you with a strap that had five-six holes in it. I ain't talking 'bout what I heard— I'm talking 'bout what I done seed.

A SENATOR SPEAKS OUT AGAINST THE KU KLUX KLAN

On March 18, 1871, United States Senator John Sherman, from Ohio, made a speech in favor of passing a law to stop acts of terror by the Ku Klux Klan.

These men are not only armed, disciplined, oath-bound members of the Confederate army, but they work in disguise; and their instruments are terror and crime. Why, sir, we are already familiar, and perhaps too familiar, with the common description of the Ku Klux Klans riding at night over a region of country, going from county to county, coming into a county town, and spreading terror all over a community; and not only that, but they endeavor to excite superstition. They pretended, I believe, in the outset to be the . . . ghosts of the Confederate dead. That was the idea they sought to give out; the ghosts of the Confederate dead were coming back to punish those who had been disloyal to the Confederate service; and they terrified men, women, and children, white and black. They excited the superstition of the ignorant negroes of the South, endeavoring to frighten them first by superstition, then by intimidation, by threats, by violence, and by murder.

Mr. President, I do not know anywhere an organization similar to this Ku Klux Klan. I have thought of the Thugs of India. They murdered, and they murdered secretly; but they did not disguise themselves while they were in the act of murder. If any Senator now, in looking over the record of crime in all ages, can tell me of . . . a band of men who combines in their acts and in their purposes more that is diabolical than this Ku Klux Klan, I should like to know where it was. They are secret, oath-bound; they murder, rob, plunder, whip, and scourge; and they commit these crimes, not upon the high and lofty, but upon the lowly, upon the poor, upon feeble men and women who are utterly defenseless. They go out at night, armed and disguised, under color of superstitious forms, and commit their work. They go over vast regions of country, carrying terror wherever they go. In all the record of human crime—and God knows it is full enough— where is there an organization against which humanity revolts more than it does against this? I know there is not a Senator here but feels that this thing ought to be put down.

A VIRGINIA NEGRO'S OPINIONS ABOUT FREEDOM

On February 3, 1866 Richard B. Hill, a freed man from Virginia was asked to tell about the life of Negroes in Virginia to a Joint Committee on Reconstruction of the United States Congress. This committee was trying to find out what were the problems of the newly freed Negroes and what the United States government could do about these problems.

Question: Where do you live?
Answer: Hampton, Virginia. . . .

Q: Can you read and write?
A: Yes, Sir.

Q: How old are you?
A: About thirty-four years.

Q: Were you ever a slave?
A: Yes, Sir.

Q: When did you become free?
A: When the proclamation was issued. . . .

Q: How did the rebels down there, about Hampton, treat the colored people?
A: The returned rebels express a desire to get along in peace if they can. There have been a few outrages out upon the roadside there. One of the returned Union soldiers was met out there and beaten very much. . . .

Q: Are they willing to pay the freedman fair wages for their work?
A: No, sir; they are not willing to pay the freedman more than from five to eight dollars a month.

Q: Do you think their labor is worth more than that generally?
A: I do, sir; because, just at this time, everything is very dear, and I do not see how people can live and support their families on those wages.

Q: State whether the black people down there are anxious to go to school.
A: Yes, sir; they are anxious to go to school; we have schools there every day that are very well filled; and we have night schools that are very well attended, both by children and aged people; they manifest a great desire for education.

Q: Who are the teachers; white or black?
A: White, sir.

Q: How are the white teachers treated by the rebels down there?
A: I guess they are not treated very well, because they have very little communication between each other. I have not heard of any threatening expression in regard to them.

Q: Did you ever hear any threats among the whites to reduce your race to slavery again?
A: They have said . . . that . . . the condition of the freedman would be very little better than that of the slaves, and that their old laws would still exist by which they would reduce them to something like bondage. That has been expressed by a great many of them. . . .

Q: How do you feel about leaving the State of Virginia and going off and residing in a community somewhere else?
A: They do not wish to leave and go anywhere else unless they are certain that the locality where they are going is healthy and that they can get along.

Q: Are they not willing to be sent back to Africa?
A: No, sir.

Q: Why not?
A: They say that they have lived here all their days, and there were stringent laws made to keep them here; and that if they could live here contented as slaves, they can live here when free.

Q: Do you not think that to be a very absurd notion?
A: No, sir; if we can get lands here and can work and support ourselves, I do not see why we should go to any place that we do not want to go to. . . .

THE FREEDMAN'S BUREAU

On October 15, 1865, Colonel E. Whittlesey gave a report to Congress about the work of the Freedman's Bureau in North Carolina. He was the assistant commissioner for that state during Reconstruction. This document was taken from *Reconstruction* which was published in 1965.

Regarding this bureau as the appointed instrument . . . to secure the rights of freedmen, I have made every effort to protect them from wrong. Suddenly set free, they were at first exhilarated by the air of liberty, and committed some excesses. To be sure of their freedom, many thought they must leave the old scenes of oppression and seek new homes. Others regarded the property accumulated by their labor as in part their own, and demanded a share of it. On the other hand, the former masters, suddenly stripped of their wealth, at first looked upon the freedmen with a mixture of hate and fear. . . . The negroes were complained of as idle, insolent, and dishonest; while they complained that they were treated with more cruelty than when they were slaves. Some were tied up and whipped without trial; some were driven from their homes without pay for their labor, without clothing or means of support; others were forbidden to leave on pain of death, and a few were shot or otherwise murdered. All officers of the bureau were directed . . . to investigate these difficulties . . . and to report more serious cases of crime to the military authorities for trial. . . . From the report of Captain James, for August, I quote the following:

> Reports had reached me of the way which David Parker, of Gates county, treated his colored people, and I determined to ascertain for myself their truth. Accordingly, last Monday, August 20, accompanied by a guard of sixty men . . . I proceeded to his residence. . . . He is very wealthy. . . . I ascertained . . . that the worst reports in regard to him were true. He had twenty-three negroes on his farm, large and small. Of these, fourteen were fieldhands; they all bore unmistakable evidence of the way they had been worked. . . . It has been his habit for years to work them from sunrise to sunset, and often long after, only stopping one hour for dinner—food always cooked for them to save time. . . .
>
> Mr. Parker told me that he had hired his people for the season: that directly after the surrender of General Lee he called them up and told them they were free; that he was better used to them than to others, and would give them board and two suits of clothing to stay with him till the 1st day of January, 1866, and one Sunday suit at the end of that time; that they consented willingly—in fact, preferred to remain with him. But from his people I learned that though he did call them up, as stated, yet when one of them demurred at the offer his son James flew at him and cuffed and kicked him; that after that they were all perfectly willing to stay; they were watched day and night; that Bob, one of the men, had been kept chained nights; that they were actually afraid to try to get away. There was no complaint of the food nor much of the clothing, but they were in constant terror of the whip. Only three days before my arrival, Bob had been stripped in the field and given fifty lashes for hitting Adam, the colored over-looker, while James Parker stood by with a gun, and told him to run if he wanted to, he had a gun there. About four weeks before, four of them who went to church and returned before sunset were treated to twenty-five lashes each. Some were beaten or whipped almost every day. Having ascertained these and other similar facts, I directed him to call them up and pay them from the first of May last up to the present time . . . and saw him pay them off then and there, allowing for clothing and medical bill. I then arrested him and his two sons. . . .

Using Historical Methods

1. What questions can be raised about the difference between a law being passed and a law being enforced? Have the three amendments to the Constitution always been enforced?

2. What facts and opinions are expressed in the document in this chapter?

3. Was Reconstruction a success according to the documents? What are your reasons for this answer?

4. What conclusions can be reached about Reconstruction after reading these documents?

5. What conclusions can be reached about the progress of the American Negro during the era of Reconstruction?

Knowing Your Vocabulary

Freedman's Bureau /ˈfrēd-məns ˈbyu̇-(ə)r-(ˌ)ō/
An agency of the federal government organized to help Negroes after their emancipation. 61

amendment /ə-ˈmen(d)-mənt/
An addition to the Constitution of the United States. 62

pardon /ˈpärd-ən/
A release from the penalty of a jail sentence or fine. 63

assassinate /ə-ˈsas-ən-ˌāt/
The murder of a high government official. 63

veto /ˈvēt-(ˌ)ō/
An objection to a law by the President of the United States. 64

carpetbagger /ˈkär-pət-bag-ər/
A northerner who came to the South during Reconstruction. 65

scalawag /ˈskal-i-ˌwag/
A southerner who cooperated with federal officials during the era of Reconstruction. 65

sharecropper /ˈshe(ə)r-ˌkräp-ər/
A person who farms land owned by someone else. Rent is paid by giving the owner a share of the crop produced. 69

Reading the Text

1. What were some of the problems the nation faced following the Civil War?

2. What solutions to these problems were offered by the Reconstruction laws and plans?

3. What were some of the major activities of the Freedman's Bureau?

4. Why did most Negroes have difficulty making progress during the era of Reconstruction?

5. Why was the suggestion that freedmen be sent to Africa a poor solution to the problems of the American Negro?

6. Do you agree or disagree with the conclusions of Frederick Douglass about Reconstruction? Why?

Identifying Names and Places

Freedman's Bureau
federal government
Thirteenth Amendment
Fourteenth Amendment
Fifteenth Amendment
Abraham Lincoln
Andrew Johnson
Radical Republicans
Thaddeus Stevens
P. B. S. Pinchback
Francis Cardozo
Knights of the Ku Klux Klan

Debating and Discussing Ideas

1. Assume that your class is the Congress of the United States at the end of the Civil War. What plan of Reconstruction would you want to make law?

2. What would be the arguments of a Ku Klux Klan member? What would be the arguments of a person opposed to the Ku Klux Klan and its ideas?

Reading Other Sources

Buckmaster, Henrietta, *Freedom Bound*, New York: Macmillan, 1965.

Catton, Bruce, *This Hallowed Ground*, Garden City, New York: Doubleday, 1962.

Cherry, Gwendolyn, *Portraits in Color: The Lives of Colorful Negro Women*, New York: Pageant, 1962.

Current, Richard N., ed., *Reconstruction: 1865—1877*, Englewood Cliffs, New Jersey: Prentice-Hall, 1965.

Fast, Howard, *Freedom Road*, New York: Pocket Books, 1946.

McCarthy, Agnes, and Lawrence Reddick, *Worth Fighting For: A History of the Negro in the United States During the Civil War and Reconstruction*, Garden City, New York: Doubleday, 1965.

4. Segregation

There's never been equality for me,
nor freedom in this "homeland of the free."

Langston Hughes
Let America Be Free Again

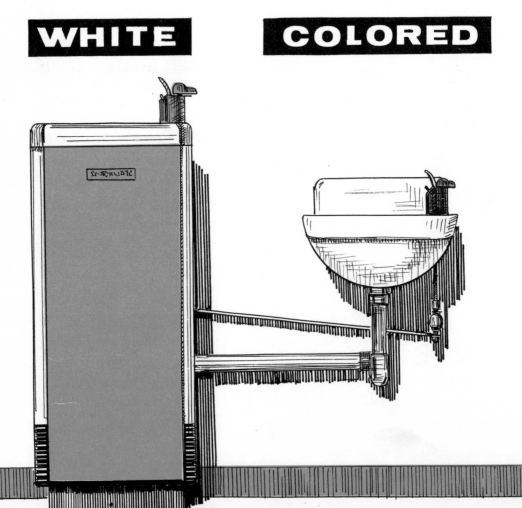

What is segregation?

During the years following Reconstruction, the way of life in the South was built on *segregation*. Negroes and whites were kept apart or segregated from one another. They used separate public facilities. Their social life was separated from one another. Some jobs were set aside for Negroes only. Negroes were forced to go to separate schools, to use separate cars in trains, to sit in special Negro sections of theaters and ball parks, and to use separate washrooms. Negroes were also forced to use separate drinking fountains, to eat in Negro restaurants, to sleep in Negro hotels, to attend separate churches, and to live in separate Negro sections of the town or city.

Each of the southern states passed laws to enforce strict segregation. It became a crime for a Negro to attend school with white people, to drink from a public water fountain marked "whites only," or to mix with white people in many other ways. It was even against the law for Negro and white people to play against one another in a sports contest. Even the benches in public parks were marked "for whites only," or "for colored only."

Signs were posted in theaters and ball parks saying, "This section reserved for whites only." Restaurants and hotels posted signs saying, "We serve only white people." Many businesses advertised that they hired only white people. Other companies would hire Negroes only to be janitors or unskilled laborers.

Negroes would never again be made to work as slaves, but segregation was a way to make them into second-class citizens. Many white people said, "It puts the Negro in his place." The Negro's place, according to these people, was at the bottom level of society.

How did segregation become part of the southern way of life?

Segregation was against the law during the Reconstruction Era. Both the Civil Rights Act of 1875 and the Fourteenth Amendment to the Constitution gave protection to Negroes against segregation. But many white people were against these laws and worked to overthrow the civil rights laws. In 1883, the United States Supreme Court declared that the Civil Rights Act was unconstitutional. This removed the law. This decision allowed segregation to spread throughout the nation. Many of the southern states made new segregation laws. By 1885, they had laws forcing Negroes to attend separate public schools. By 1890, laws were passed all over the South to force Negroes and whites to remain apart from each other. No longer could the two races live, work, or play together. These new laws formed two separate societies in the United States, one for whites, and one for Negroes.

What was the *Plessy vs. Ferguson* case?

In 1896, the United States Supreme Court once again supported segregation in the case of *Plessy vs. Ferguson*. Homer Plessy, a Negro, had purchased a train ticket to travel between two cities in Louisiana. Plessy entered a passenger car that was reserved for whites only. He sat down in the car. The state of Louisiana had a law that said all railway companies carrying passengers in Louisiana must have separate cars for white and Negro passengers. The conductor ordered Plessy to sit in the car reserved for Negroes. Plessy refused and was arrested. Later he was convicted of breaking the law of the state of Louisiana. Plessy *appealed* this conviction to the United States Supreme Court. An appeal is to have the case heard again in a higher court. Plessy said that the segregation laws of Louisiana should be declared unconstitutional because they conflicted with the Fourteenth Amendment to the United States Constitution. This amendment says that all people shall have equal protection of the law. Plessy argued that segregation laws took away certain rights from Negroes. The majority of the U.S. Supreme Court did not agree with Plessy. They voted to uphold the segregation laws. They said that public facilities could be segregated if the facilities provided for Negroes were equal to the facilities provided for the white people. Segregation became stronger than ever after this decision by the U.S. Supreme Court.

Homer Plessy was ordered out of a white railroad car. His refusal resulted in a famous Supreme Court decision.

FOR WHITE ONLY

How were voting rights taken away?

An important part of the segregation system was to take away the rights of Negroes to participate in government. Without the right to vote or to be candidates for public office, Negroes were powerless to change the segregation laws. Voting is the basic right of an individual in a democracy, and without this right, Negroes were left helpless at the hands of the white majority. Several states in the South discovered means by which this basic right of voting in an election could be taken away. Negroes were powerless to stop this course of events.

The Fifteenth Amendment to the Constitution says, "The right of citizens of the United States to vote shall not be denied . . . by any State on account of race, color, or previous condition of servitude." The southern states, however, used many unusual and unjust methods to get around this amendment. For example, an Alabama law required all voters to have "good character." It was easy for Alabama to charge that Negroes did not have "good character" and to take away their right to vote. Some states required voters to pass a *literacy test*. This test required voters to be able to read and write. Often the test was made harder for Negroes than for whites. In 1890 Mississippi passed a law that prevented anyone from voting who could not read and show a satisfactory understanding of the state constitution. This voter's test was often used unfairly to prevent Negroes from voting. Most southern states also required people to pay a *poll tax*. This was a certain amount of money that had to be paid before a person was allowed to vote. This stopped many poor Negroes and also poor whites from voting. They were too poor to pay the poll tax.

A new method to keep Negroes from voting was used in Louisiana in 1898. It was called the *Grandfather Clause*. It said that anyone whose father or grandfather was qualified to vote as of January 1, 1867, was permanently registered as a legal voter.

All other people had to be property owners or pass a test in order to vote. Because the only fathers and grandfathers who were registered voters in 1867 were white, the only voters now allowed were also white. All other people would either have to be property owners or would have to pass a literacy test given by the state of Louisiana.

Terror, violence, and threats were used to keep many Negroes from voting. Beatings, house burnings, dismissal from jobs, and even murder were commonly used to prevent Negro voting. Although the state governments of the South had nothing to do with these acts of terror, they usually did little to stop them.

The attitude of the federal government also had changed since the days of Reconstruction. Congress and the President no longer seemed to care that some states did not obey the Fourteenth and Fifteenth Amendments to the U.S. Constitution.

Most Negroes decided it was more important to protect their jobs, homes, and lives than to vote. They stayed home on election days. In 1896 there were 130,344 Negroes registered to vote in Louisiana. By 1900, only 5,320 Negroes were still registered in that state.

In Alabama in 1900 there were 181,471 Negroes of voting age, but only 3,000 of them were registered to vote. This loss of voting rights continued until the 1960's.

Even public parks had separate benches for whites and Negroes.

Was segregation practiced in other sections of the United States?

Segregation was never practiced in the northern or western states as completely as it was in the South. In the North and the West, Negroes often were forced to live in one section of the city. Often they were not served at certain hotels or restaurants. But there was no such thing as separate washrooms or drinking fountains. Most important, Negroes were not stopped from voting in the states of the North and the West. Also of great importance was the fact that most schools were not segregated in the northern or the western states.

Negroes and whites usually went to school together.

Why did segregation become part of the southern way of life?

Many white southerners defended segregation as strongly as other white southerners had once defended slavery. The arguments for segregation sounded very much like the arguments for slavery. They said Negroes were not ready to accept the responsibility of voting or holding public office. They pointed out that most Negroes were not educated and were not fit for leadership roles. Negroes, therefore had to be taken care of, had

The armed forces of the United States were segregated until President Truman ended this practice.

Many organizations and businesses have been picketed and boycotted because of their segregation practices.

to be shown the right way to live, and had to be taught by white people who knew what was good for them. Some segregationists said that Negroes might be able to take care of themselves at a future date. Once this happened, full freedom and equality would be theirs. They felt, however, this day was a long way off. They told Negroes to be patient and to listen to what their white friends told them and asked them.

These believers in segregation used the events of Reconstruction to support their arguments. To them, Reconstruction was a terrible time of troubles and confusion. This confusion was caused by giving Negroes responsibilities they could not handle.

Segregationists were determined that this would not happen again.

Some Negroes were elected to public office during Reconstruction. Segregationists were determined not to allow this to happen again. But in many counties of the South, Negroes outnumbered whites. In a free election the Negro candidate would win. The only way the segregationists could stop Negro participation in government was to stop Negroes from voting.

During Reconstruction some Negro public officials were corrupt and inefficient. Others were not able to do their jobs properly because they were not educated and had no experience in government.

Southern sharecroppers were always in debt. They had no possibility to improve their lives.

Some white public officials were also corrupt and inefficient. The Negro public officials were no better than other public officials during this time. The Reconstruction governments were no better and no worse than state governments in other sections of the country. In spite of all of the problems, the Reconstruction governments made solid contributions to the progress of the South.

Some segregationists wanted to try to help Negroes improve their education and their job skills. Most segregationists wanted to deprive Negroes of their rights. They wanted to keep Negroes ignorant and helpless in order to use them as a cheap supply of labor. Too much education was dangerous, they felt, because it would allow Negroes to see and understand that their place in life was not only as an uneducated laborer.

Why did segregation cause Negroes to migrate from the South?

There has been a continuous migration of Negroes from the South to the North for the past one hundred years. In 1860 only about one out of every twelve Negroes lived outside the South. Today almost half of all Negroes live outside the South. Most of these Negro migrants have moved to large northern cities, such as Chicago, New York, and Los Angeles.

Thousands of southern Negroes migrated to the North. Many of them could not find jobs and were forced to receive welfare payments.

In 1860 New York had a Negro population of 12,569. Today over one million Negro people live in New York City. The city of Chicago has more Negro residents than the entire former Confederate state of Arkansas. During the period 1950 to 1960, there was a total of 1,283,100 Negro people who left the South for the northern cities and towns.

Better jobs and a better way of life were the reasons for this migration. For Negroes in the South, wages were low, living standards were low, and chances for a better job were few. The average southern Negro share-cropper lived in a small, poorly built, and poorly furnished house. His hours of work were long and hard. His diet was poor, his health was bad, and his life expectancy was short. Usually his debts were greater than his income.

Compare the states of the South with other states in the United States. In 1902 farm workers in South Carolina received $10.79 per month as compared to $26.13 per month in New York. In 1960 the *median* yearly income for Negroes in Mississippi was $724. This means one-half of the 915,000 Negroes made more than $724 per year, and one-half made less than $724 per year. In Illinois the 1960 median income for Negroes was $4,590. In 1964 the median yearly income for Negroes in all of the southern states was $2,520.

Greater educational opportunities for Negroes existed outside the South. The segregated schools of the South were supposed to be equal. But in most cases, the Negro schools were not as new or as well equipped as the white schools. This was because less money was spent on the schools for Negroes. In 1898 Florida was spending $5.92 for the education of each white child. Florida only spent $2.27 for the education of each Negro child that same year. In Adams County, Mississippi in 1900, $2.00 was spent for each Negro child and $22.25 for each white child. In 1940, $50.14 was spent per white child in the South as compared to $21.54 per Negro child. In 1961 the state of Mississippi spent $81.86 for the education of each white child and $21.77 for each Negro child.

The quality of education for Negroes in the South was very poor. There were few if any facilities provided for a good education.

85

LYNCHINGS
1882-1951

STATE	WHITE	NEGRO		STATE	WHITE	NEGRO
Alabama	48	299		Nevada	6	0
Arizona	31	0		New Jersey	0	3
Arkansas	58	226		New Mexico	33	1
California	41	2		New York	1	1
Colorado	66	2		North Carolina	15	84
Delaware	0	1		North Dakota	13	3
Florida	25	257		Ohio	10	16
Georgia	39	491		Oklahoma	82	40
Idaho	20	0		Oregon	20	1
Illinois	15	19		Pennsylvania	2	6
Indiana	33	14		South Carolina	4	156
Iowa	17	2		South Dakota	27	0
Kansas	35	19		Tennessee	47	204
Kentucky	63	142		Texas	141	352
Louisiana	56	335		Utah	6	2
Maryland	2	27		Virginia	17	83
Michigan	7	1		Washington	25	1
Minnesota	5	4		West Virginia	20	28
Mississippi	40	534		Wisconsin	6	0
Missouri	53	69		Wyoming	30	5
Montana	82	2				
Nebraska	52	5		TOTAL	1,293	3,437

Did violence help cause the Negro migration from the South?

Another important cause of the Negro migration from the South was lack of personal safety and security. Negroes regularly faced the threat of *lynch mobs* and riots. These mobs were made up of people who took the law into their own hands and hanged or shot Negroes who were accused of breaking the law. Sometimes these victims of the mob were guilty of some crime. Often they had broken no law, but they had no way of proving their innocence. Lynch mobs permitted no fair trials and no legal defense for their victims. Negroes could not expect nor did they receive equal justice under the laws of the southern states.

Mobs of white rioters who would injure or kill Negroes and who would destroy property owned by Negroes were an ever present danger to many Negroes in the South. The South's largest riot happened in Atlanta, Georgia in 1906. On September 22, 1906, newspapers reported that four Negro men had attacked some white women. This report angered many white people. They joined together to attack every Negro they saw. Innocent Negroes were dragged from wagons and trains and beaten. The following day gangs of white people came to a Negro suburb of Atlanta and began to burn houses and attack Negro people. Four Negroes were killed and thousands of dollars worth of property was destroyed.

What special problems have Negroes faced outside the South?

Although Negroes have found better opportunities outside the South, they have also found many problems and disappointments. As Negroes moved into the large cities of the North, they had trouble finding suitable places in which to live. Most of these people had no money when they arrived in the city. They could only afford to live in the cheaper and more run-down areas of the city. Many who could afford better housing were not allowed to live in other areas of the city. White property owners refused to sell or to rent homes to Negroes in the better parts of the city. Some white people would use threats of force to stop Negroes from moving into their neighborhoods. Many Negro families moving into an all white section of town were often greeted by an angry mob of whites. Some Negroes had their homes bombed. Usually these Negroes would move away because the white people would not let them live in peace and safety. This has meant that almost all Negroes have had to live together in the same run-down section of the city. These areas are called *ghettos*.

The public schools in ghettos are often very old and overcrowded. Other public facilities in the ghettos, such as parks, playgrounds, and libraries, are often not as good as the facilities in other areas of the city.

As in all large city slums, the crime rate is high, Much violence takes place on the streets after dark. The central Harlem section of New York City is a good example of a northern Negro ghetto.

POPULATION DENSITY OF HARLEM

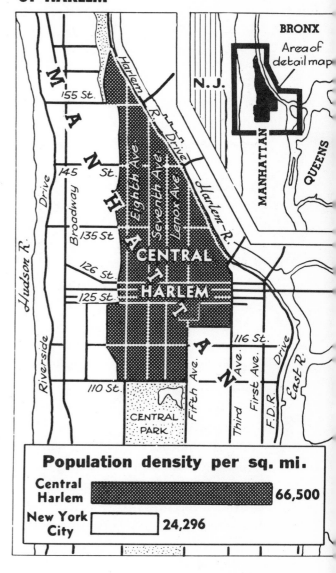

Population density per sq. mi.	
Central Harlem	66,500
New York City	24,296

HARLEM-FACTORS BEHIND THE NEGRO DISCONTENT

Low Income
Median annual family income.

Central Harlem

 $3,995

New York City

 $6,100

High Unemployment
Per cent of work force unemployed, 1963

Central Harlem

15%

New York City

5%

The graphs on this page show many of the problems faced by the Negro people who live in Harlem. The problems of the people in Central Harlem are very similar to the problems of people in other large city ghettos in the North. People living in Harlem suffer from the problems of low income, high unemployment rates, poor housing, high crime rates, and a high rate of infant deaths.

Many Negro migrants to the northern and western cities have been unable to find steady employment. Many are forced to depend on state and city welfare payments in order to stay alive. Nearly one-third of all Chicago mothers receiving aid-to-dependent children welfare funds are Negroes born in Mississippi. Many southern migrants to the cities have had great difficulty becoming accustomed to their new way of life.

One reason for the high unemployment rate is Negroes usually lose when they compete for jobs with white people. The Negroes usually have less education and fewer job skills than white job seekers. They also face the possibility of discrimination by employers. They often are the last to be hired and the first to be fired. This is why the median income for Negroes is about $2,000 less than it is for white people.

Negroes outside the South have also suffered from mobs and white violence. Much of this violence has happened after a Negro has been accused of committing a crime. The riot of 1908 in Springfield, Illinois is a typical example. A white woman claimed that a Negro named George Richardson had attacked her. Later she said that Richardson had done nothing to her. Meantime, mobs of white people were angered and began to destroy Negro homes. The mob burned a Negro barber shop and then lynched the Negro owner. Later this mob lynched an eighty-four year old Negro man. More than seventy other people were injured before the state militia stopped this riot.

Another terrible riot started in 1919 in Chicago when a Negro boy swam into an area of Lake Michigan that was used only by white people. White people on the beach started throwing stones at him. He drowned. Fights between Negroes and whites started because of this incident. The fighting spread to various parts of the city. The riot lasted for almost a week. The mayor was forced to call the state militia to restore order. Thirty-eight people died as a result of the riot, fifteen white and twenty-three Negro. Five hundred thirty-seven people were injured in this riot.

How has segregation affected the progress of the American Negro?

The segregation system robbed Negroes of their civil rights. They lost equal protection under the law. This violated the Fourteenth Amendment. Many lost the right to vote. This violated the Fifteenth Amendment.

The loss of these civil rights was a severe handicap. Segregated facilities were supposed to follow the rule of "separate but equal." This rule had been set forth by the United States Supreme Court in 1896. In most cases, however, the Negro public facilities were not as good as the facilities for white people. Segregation was also an insult to Negroes. This system suggested that Negroes could not associate with white people because they were not as good.

Poor Housing
Per cent of housing below standard.
Central Harlem
49%
New York City
15%

High Rate of Delinquency
Offenses per 1,000 population.
Central Harlem
109.3
New York City
46.5

High Infant Mortality
Deaths per 1,000 births.
Central Harlem
45.3
New York City
26.3

High Use of Narcotics
Rate per 10,000 population.
Central Harlem
40
New York City
5

Segregation made a low *caste* out of the Negroes in America. A caste is a group of people that is kept apart from other people. A Negro's dark skin was the sign of membership in this low caste. No matter how much a Negro accomplished, no matter how great or wealthy he became, he was never allowed to forget that he belonged to the lowest caste. This caste membership meant he was kept from doing many things. Even if he was a star baseball or football player, he could never play with whites on a professional team. Even if he was a respected businessman, he could not sleep in certain hotels or eat in certain restaurants. Even if he was a minister of a church, he could not attend white religious services.

Jesse Owens was one of the greatest track stars in the United States. He won four gold medals in the Olympics of 1936.

Gale Sayers, halfback for the Chicago Bears, makes a move to elude several other players.

Segregation gave a low status to all Negroes. It greatly limited their roles in American life. Most Negroes lacked the skills for any but the lowest paying and the hardest jobs. They had few opportunities for advancement. Only slightly more than half of all American Negroes could read and write in 1900. There were only 2,000 Negro doctors, 21,000 Negro teachers, and 300 Negro journalists out of a total Negro population of eight million. This small number of Negroes gave living proof that Negroes could play leadership roles. They could make progress if they were given a chance. Unfortunately, many Negroes today are still not given that opportunity.

A NEGRO IS "PUT IN HIS PLACE"

Richard Wright has written many famous books and stories about the Negro people. He has been called one of the greatest Negro writers of the twentieth century. He was born in 1908 on a plantation near Natchez, Mississippi. Later he lived in Memphis, Tennessee. In 1934 Wright went to Chicago, Illinois and began to earn his living as a writer. Most of his stories are based on personal experiences as a Negro living in a segregated society. He died in Paris, France in 1960. This description was taken from *Uncle Tom's Children* which was published in 1936.

My first job was with an optical company in Jackson, Mississippi. The morning I applied I stood straight and neat before the boss, answering all the questions with sharp yessirs and nosirs. I was very careful to pronounce my sirs distinctly, in order that he might know that I was polite, that I knew where I was, and that I knew he was a white man. I wanted that job very badly. . . . My wages were five dollars a week.

I worked hard, trying to please. For the first month I got along O.K. Both Pease and Morrie seemed to like me. But one thing was missing. And I kept thinking about it. I was not learning anything and nobody was volunteering to help me. Thinking they had forgotten that I was to learn something about the mechanics of grinding lenses, I asked Morrie one day to tell me about the work. He grew red.

"What yuh tryin' t' do, nigger, get smart?" he said.
"Naw, I ain' tryin' t' git smart," I said.
"Well, don't if yuh know whut's good for yuh!"

I was puzzled. Maybe he just doesn't want to help me, I thought. I went to Pease.
"Say, are yuh crazy?" Pease asked me, his gray eyes growing hard.

I spoke out, reminding him that the boss had said I was to be given a chance to learn something.
"Nigger, you think you're white, don't you?"
"Naw, sir!"
"Well you're acting mighty like it!"
"But, Mr. Pease, the boss said. . . ."

Pease shook his fist in my face.

"This is white man's work around here, and you better watch yourself!" From then on they changed toward me. . . . When I told the folks at home what had happened, they called me a fool. They told me that I must never again attempt to exceed my boundaries. When you are working for white folks, they said, you got to "stay in your place" if you want to keep working.

NEGRO LIFE IN ALABAMA

Booker T. Washington founded Tuskegee Institute in Alabama and developed it into a famous school. Before starting his work at Tuskegee, he traveled around Alabama to find out how the Negro people lived. The following descriptions were taken from Washington's autobiography, *Up From Slavery*.

I reached Tuskegee . . . early in June, 1881. The first month I spent in finding accomodations for the school, and in travelling through Alabama, examining into the actual life of the people. . . . The most of my travelling was done over the country roads, with a mule and a cart or a mule and a buggy wagon for conveyance. I ate and slept with the people, in their little cabins. I saw their farms, their schools, their churches. Since, in the case of the most of these visits, there had been no notice given in advance that a stranger was expected, I had the advantage of seeing the real, everyday life of the people. In the plantation districts I found that, as a rule the whole family slept in one room, and that in addition to the immediate family there sometimes were relatives, or others not related to the family, who slept in the same room. . . . Rarely was there any place provided in the cabin where one could bathe even the face and hands, but usually some provision was made for this outside the house, in the yard.

The common diet of the people was fat pork and corn bread. At times I have eaten in cabins where they had only corn bread and "black-eye peas" cooked in plain water. The people seemed to have no other idea than to live on this fat meat and corn bread—the meat, and the meal of which the bread was made, having been bought at a high price at a store in town, notwithstanding the fact that the land all about the cabin homes could easily have been made to produce nearly every kind of garden vegetable that is raised anywhere in the country. Their one object seemed to be to plant nothing but cotton; and in many cases cotton was planted up to the very door of cabin. . . .

In most cases, when the family got up in the morning . . . the wife would put a piece of meat in a frying-pan and put a lump of dough in a "skillet," as they called it. . . . Frequently the husband would take his bread and meat in his hand and start for the field, eating as he walked. The mother would sit down in a corner and eat her breakfast, perhaps from a plate and perhaps directly from the "skillet" or frying-pan, while the children would eat their portion of the bread and meat while running about the yard. At certain seasons of the year, when meat was scarce, it was rarely that the children who were not old enough or strong enough to work in the fields would have the luxury of meat.

The breakfast over, and with practically no attention given to the house, the whole family would, as a general thing, proceed to the cotton-field. Every child that was large enough to carry a hoe was put to work, and the baby—for usually there was at least one baby—would be laid down at the end of the cotton row, so that its mother could give it a certain amount of attention when she had finished chopping her row. The noon meal and the supper were taken in much the same way as the breakfast.

All the days of the family would be spent after much this same routine, except Saturday and Sunday. On Saturday the whole family would spend at least half a day and often a whole day, in town. The idea in going to town was, I suppose, to do shopping, but all the shopping that the whole family had money for could have been attended to in ten minutes by one person. Still, the whole family remained in town for most of the day, spending the greater part of the time in standing on the streets, the women, too often, sitting about somewhere smoking or dipping snuff. Sunday was usually spent in going to some big meeting. With few exceptions, I found that the crops were mortgaged in the counties where I went, and that the most of the colored farmers were in debt. The state had not been able to build schoolhouses in the country districts, and, as a rule, the schools were taught in churches or in log cabins. More than once, while on my journeys, I found that there was no provision made in the house used for school purposes for heating the building during the winter, and consequently a fire had to be built in the yard, and teacher and pupils passed in and out of the house as they got cold or warm. With few exceptions, I found the teachers in these country schools to be miserably poor in preparation for their work, and poor in moral character. The schools were in session from three to five months. There was practically no apparatus in the schoolhouses, except that occasionally there was a rough blackboard. I recall that one day I went into a schoolhouse—or rather into an abandoned log cabin that was being used as a schoolhouse—and found five pupils who were studying a lesson from one book. Two of these, on the front seat, were using the book between them; behind these were two others peeping over the shoulders of the first two, and behind the four was a fifth little fellow who was peeping over the shoulders of all four....

I met some very interesting characters during my travels. I remember that I asked one colored man, who was about sixty years old, to tell me something of his history. He said that he had been born in Virginia, and sold into Alabama in 1845. I asked him how many were sold at the same time. He said, "There were five of us; myself and brother and three mules."

THE KU KLUX KLAN TERROR

In 1871 at Columbia, South Carolina, members of the Ku Klux Klan were being tried for the murder of Jim Williams, a Negro. Gadsden Steel, a Negro, gave evidence at the trial.

Gadsden Steel, a witness for the prosecution, being duly sworn, testified as follows:

Question: Now tell the jury about the Ku Klux Klan coming to your house last March, on the night that Jim Williams was killed; what they said and did, and what you said, and all about it.

Answer: They came to my house about ten o'clock, and I was in bed at the time; and I was asleep; and my wife she heard them before I did, and she shook me and woke me, and told me she heard a mighty riding and walking, and said I had better get up, she thought it was Ku Klux. I jumped up and put on my pantaloons, and stepped to the door, and looked out, and very close to the door I seen the men, and I stepped right back into the house; so when they knocked the door open they couldn't see me; and they came in and called for me to give up my gun, and I says I has no gun; and when I spoke they all grabbed me, and taken me out into the yard.

Question: What sort of looking people were they?

Answer: They was all disguised; as far as I could see—they was all disguised, and struck me three licks over the head, and jobbed the blood out of me, right forninst my eye, with a pistol, and down by my mouth here....

Question: Repeat, if you please, what that man told you when he let you go. . . .

Answer: . . . they said, "You go home and go to bed, and if you are not there in the morning when we come along, the next time we call, we will kill you. We are going to kill all you . . . niggers that vote these Radical tickets. We are going to kill Jim, and are going to kill all these . . . niggers that vote the Radical ticket."

SEPARATE BUT EQUAL

In the case of *Plessy vs. Ferguson*, 1896, the United States Supreme Court decided in favor of segregation. The majority of the court said that Negroes could be forced to use separate facilities from whites if these facilities were equal to those used by the white people. Justice Henry Brown wrote the majority opinion of the court. But Justice John Marshall Harlan, who was a strong defender of civil rights, disagreed with the majority opinion of the court.

Mr. Justice Brown: The object of the (Fourteenth) amendment was undoubtedly to enforce the absolute equality of the two races before the law, but in the nature of things it could not have been intended to abolish distinctions based upon color, or to enforce social, as distinguished from political equality. . . . Laws permitting, and even requiring, their separation in places where they are liable to be brought into contact do not necessarily imply the inferiority of either race to the other. . . . The most common instance of this is connected with the establishment of separate schools for white and colored children. . . .

Gauged by this standard, we cannot say that a law which . . . required the separation of the two races in public conveyances is unreasonable. . . .

We consider the underlying fallacy of the plaintiff's argument to consist in the assumption that the enforced separation of the two races stamps the colored race with a badge of inferiority. . . . The argument also assumes that social prejudices may be overcome by legislation, and that equal rights cannot be secured by the negro except by an enforced commingling of the two races. We cannot accept this. . . . If the two races are to meet upon terms of social equality, it must be the result of natural affinities, a mutual appreciation of each other's merits and a voluntary consent of individuals. . . . If the civil and political rights of both races be equal one cannot be inferior to the other civilly or politically. If one race be inferior to the other socially, the Constitution of the United States cannot put them upon the same plane.

Mr. Justice Harlan: If a white man and a black man choose to occupy the same public conveyance on a public highway, it is their right to do so, and no government, proceeding along on grounds of race, can prevent it without infringing the personal liberty of each. . . .

The white race deems itself to be the dominant race in this country. . . . But in the view of the Constitution, in the eye of the law, there is in this country no superior, dominant ruling class of citizens. There is no caste here. Our Constitution is colorblind, and neither knows nor tolerates classes among citizens. In respect of civil rights, all citizens are equal before the law. The humblest is the peer of the most powerful. The law regards man as man, and takes no account of his surroundings or of his color. . . . It is, therefore, to be regretted that this high tribunal . . . has reached the conclusion that it is competent for a State to regulate the enjoyment by citizens of their civil rights solely upon the basis of race. . . .

It is scarcely just to say that a colored person should not object to occupying a public coach assigned to his own race. He does not object, nor, perhaps, would he object to separate coaches for his race, if his rights under the law were recognized. But he objects, and ought never to cease objecting to the proposition, that citizens of the white and black races can be adjudged criminals because they sit, or claim the right to sit, in the same public coach on a public highway.

The . . . separation of citizens on a basis of race, while they are on a public highway, is a badge of servitude wholly inconsistent with the civil freedom and the equality before the law established by the Constitution. . . .

We boast of the freedom enjoyed by our people above all other peoples. But it is difficult to reconcile the boast with a state of the law which, practically, puts the brand of servitude and degradation upon a large class of our fellow-citizens, our equals before the law. The thin disguise of "equal" accomodations for passengers in railroad coaches will not mislead any one, nor atone for the wrong this day done.

NEGRO MIGRATION

Many thousands of Negroes have migrated to other parts of the country because of their hatred for the segregation system of the South. This migration began on a large scale during the 1870's. A Senate committee was appointed to find out the reasons for this migration. Among the many Negroes which they questioned were Henry Adams and John H. Johnson.

Question: Now, Mr. Adams . . . tell us in a few words what you believe to be the causes of these people going away?

Answer: Well, the cause is, in my judgment, and from what information I have received, and that I have seen with my own eyes—it is because the largest majority of the people, of the white people, that held us as slaves, treats our people so bad in many respects that it is impossible for them to stand it. Now, in a great many parts of that country there our people most as well be slaves as to be free. . . .

Question: (To John H. Johnson) What did the Negroes give as their reasons for migrating?

Answer: They stated that they had no security for life, limb, or property; that they worked year in and year out, and, notwithstanding they raised good crops, they were at the end of the year in debt; that they were charged exorbitant prices for provisions, and all these things kept them down and in debt. The high prices charged them for lands and the denial of their rights as citizens induced them to leave and seek a genial spot where they could have an opportunity to build up themselves and their families. Some of them states that they had been on plantations alongside of theirs where men were shot down for political purposes. . . . If they were treated as human beings, to say nothing of their citizenship they would remain. The South is the home of the colored man. . . . If he had his rights under the Constitution he would remain. If he were allowed the opportunity of purchasing a homestead in the South he would remain. If he were encouraged in his efforts to get along he would remain.

A SOUTHERNER DEFENDS THE SEGREGATION SYSTEM

Hilary A. Herbert, a Democratic Congressman from Alabama during the 1890's, was one of many white Southern leaders who publicly defended the segregation system. His ideas on segregation were written in *Why The Solid South*, which was published in 1890. Herbert's ideas had a great influence on many Americans in all parts of the country and helped to make the segregation system of the South acceptable to northern whites.

The days during which the reconstruction governments ruled in the several Southern states were the darkest that ever shrouded any portion of our country. . . .

. . . there was, in the scenes (of Reconstruction) . . . nothing but wretchedness and humiliation, and shame, and crime begetting crime. . . .

The domination of the black man's party . . . meant ruin. To avert ruin white men united; and then came a struggle, the issue of which was in all the States the same. It could not anywhere be doubtful. The race against which the negro had allowed himself to be arrayed has never yet met its master. It could not go down before the African. . . .

But victor though the white man was, no one could regret the enforced conflict more than did the people of the South. And they set to work at once to make a kindly use of their victories. Under the laws passed by Southern white men the negroes in every Southern State are far more prosperous than they ever were under the rule of those who claimed to be their especial friends.

There is no large body of men of African descent anywhere in the world superior in morals, equal in industry and intelligence, or as well to do as the negroes in the Southern States of this Union. Their condition is . . . . better than that of their brethren in such countries as Hayti, where the colored man reigns supreme. . . .

So in every State in the South the effort is being made, and successfully, too, to better the condition of the negro, to train him in the duties of citizenship. These States are expending many millions per annum for educational purposes. . . .

When the negro was a slave the white men of the South made it unlawful to teach him to read. This was to prevent his learning the lesson of the insurrection which certain writers in the abolition press were seeking to instill into his mind. The Southern whites then desired to keep the negro in slavery. Now that he is free these same whites are taxing themselves to fit him for freedom.

NORTHERN RACISM

Often Negroes who migrated to the North found disappointment instead of the new freedom of which they had dreamed. This document shows the difficulty faced by Negro families when they moved into a white neighborhood. It also shows the strong feelings of hatred which some northern white people have against all Negroes. This document was taken from *The Negro in Chicago*. This book was written by the Chicago Committee on Race Relations and was published in 1922.

In 1913 S. P. Motley, a Negro, and his wife purchased a building at 5230 Maryland Avenue through a white agent, and on March 15, 1913, the family moved in. For four years they lived there without molestation save the silent resentment of neighbors and open objection to the presence of Negro children in the streets. On July 1, 1917, without warning or threat, a bomb was exploded in the vestibule of the house, and the front of the building was blown away. The damage amounted to $1,000. Police arrived . . . ten minutes after the explosion. No clews were found and no arrests were made. The owner of the building was bitterly opposed to Negroes and was a member of an organization which was seeking to keep Negroes out of the district.

Some time after this incident it was rumored that Motley was planning to purchase the building adjacent. At 4:00 A.M. June 4, 1919, a dynamite bomb was exploded under the front of the house adjacent. . . . No clews were found and no arrests were made. . . .

A resident in . . . (an integrated neighborhood) said: "A colored family lives next door north of me, and you'll be surprised when I tell you that I haven't been able to open my bedroom window on that side to air that room for three years. I couldn't think of unlocking the windows because their window is so near somebody could easily step across into this house. It's awful to have to live in such fear of your life."

When asked if she considered her neighbors so dangerous as that, she said: "Well, no, the woman seems pretty nice. I see her out in the back yard occasionally and bid her the time of day out of charity. You can't help but pity them, so I am charitable and speak. Where the danger really is, is that you never know who's in their house, they bring such trash to the neighborhood, even if they are good and decent. How do I know what kind of people this woman next door associates with? There's awful-looking people sit on the front porch sometimes. Why, I couldn't sit on my porch on the hottest day because I'd be afraid they would come out any minute. And what white person will sit on a porch next door to a porch with black ones on it? Not me, anyhow, nor you either I hope."

Another resident said: "I have nothing against the black man as a black man. He comes into my place of business (drug-store) and I sell him. Not many come in, as there aren't a lot of colored people around here. But I don't want to live with niggers any more than you or any other white person does. People who say, 'I like the colored people and don't see why others can't get along with them' don't talk practical common sense. . . .

"Niggers are different from whites and always will be, and that is why white people don't want them around. But the only thing we can do, it seems to me, is to make the best of it and live peaceably with them. The North can never do what the South does—down there it is pure autocracy. I might say like Russia."

BLACK LIKE ME

In 1960 John Howard Griffin, a white man from Texas, used a dye to darken his skin. He then traveled through the South disguised as a Negro. He wanted to learn what it was like for a Negro to live under the segregation system. Later he described his travels in the book *Black Like Me*. This book was published in 1960.

. . . the Negro is treated not even as a second-class citizen, but as a tenth-class one. His day-to-day living is a reminder of his inferior status. He does not become calloused to these things—the polite rebuffs when he seeks better employment; hearing himself referred to as nigger, coon, jigaboo; having to bypass available rest-room facilities or eating facilities to find one specified for him. Each new reminder strikes at the raw-spot, deepens the wound. . . .

In the bus station lobby, I looked for signs indicating a colored waiting room, but saw none. I walked up to the ticket counter. When the lady ticket-seller saw me, her otherwise attractive face turned sour, violently so. This look was so unexpected and so unprovoked I was taken aback. "What do you want?" she snapped. Taking care to pitch my voice to politeness, I asked about the next bus to Hattiesburg. She answered rudely and glared at me with such loathing I know I was receiving what the Negroes call "the hate stare." It is far more than the look of disapproval one occasionally gets. This was so exaggeratedly hateful I would have been amused if I had not been so surprised.

I framed the words in my mind: "Pardon me, but have I done something to offend you?" But I realized I had done nothing—my color offended her. . . .

With almost an hour before bus departure, I turned away and looked for a place to sit. The large, handsome room was almost empty. No other Negroes were there, and I dared not take a seat unless I saw some other Negro also seated.

Once again a "hate stare" drew my attention like a magnet. It came from a middle-aged, heavy-set, well-dressed white man. He sat a few yards away, fixing his eyes on me. Nothing can describe the withering horror of this. You feel lost, sick at heart before such unmasked hatred, not so much because it threatens you as because it shows humans in such inhuman light. . . .

A Negro porter sidled over to me. . . . "Where am I supposed to go?" I asked him. . . . "Go outside and around the corner of the building. You'll find the room."

The white man continued to stare, his mouth twisted with loathing as he turned his head to watch me move away. In the colored waiting room . . . I took the last empty seat.

Using Historical Methods

1. Which documents in this chapter explain the causes of the segregasion system? What are the causes?

2. Which documents in this chapter explain the results of the segregation system? What are the results?

3. Give historical evidence for some of the results of segregation that are mentioned in this chapter.

4. Place all of the documents in chronological order. Are there any conclusions you can make after studying the documents in chronological order?

5. What are the conclusions of Justice Brown in the *Plessy vs. Ferguson* case? What are the conclusions of Justice Harlan?

6. What conclusions can be reached from the facts regarding state aid to education?

7. What questions can be raised regarding the high rate of violence and crime in the ghetto of a large city?

8. According to the documents, what would be the values of a white segregationist? What things would he think are important?

Knowing Your Vocabulary

segregation /ˌseg-ri-'gā-shən/
The practice of separating Negroes and whites in the United States. 79

appeal /ə-'pē(ə)l/
To have a case heard again by a higher court. 80

literacy test /'lit-ə-rə-sē- 'test/
A test to determine if a person can read and write. 81

poll tax /'pōl-'taks/
A tax or money payment before a person is allowed to vote. 81

Grandfather Clause /'gran(d)- ˌfäth-ər-'klòz/
A law that said if your father or grandfather was registered to vote in 1867, you will also be permanently registered to vote. 81

median /'mēd-ē-ən/
The amount where one-half the population is higher, and one-half the population is lower. 85

lynch mob /'linch- 'mäb/
A mob that hangs or shoots people without a fair trial. 86

ghetto /'get-(ˌ)ō/
An area of the city where only one kind of people live. 87

caste /'kast/
A group of people who are kept apart from other people. 90

Reading the Text

1. What are the similarities of the role of Negroes during the era of Reconstruction and during the era of segregation?

2. Why did segregation become an accepted way of life in the United States?

3. How was segregation in the West and the North different from segregation in the South?

4. What were some of the main causes of Negro migration from the South?

5. What is the relationship between segregation and racism?

6. What major laws did segregation violate?

7. What were some of the main public facilities that were segregated?

8. How did some of the states take away the voting rights of Negroes? Explain how each system worked or operated?

9. What are some reasons why the crime rate is higher in a ghetto than in other areas of a city?

10. What effects does a ghetto have on the people who live in a ghetto?

11. Compare each of the three riots mentioned in this chapter. What are the similarities?

12. What are some of the reasons why there were so few Negro professional people?

Identifying Names and Places

"in his place"
Plessy vs. Ferguson
literacy test
poll tax
Grandfather Clause
separate but equal
Atlanta riot 1906
Chicago riot 1919
aid-to-dependent children
Harlem
Richard Wright
Booker T. Washington
Justice Harlan
Justice Brown

Debating and Discussing Ideas

1. Give a complete argument and defense of the segregation system. Why is it necessary? How does it work? What does it hope to accomplish?

2. Give a complete argument against the segregation system. Why is it wrong? What harm does it do? Why is it unconstitutional?

3. What effects on people do segregation and the ghetto have? Why do these effects cause people to behave in certain ways?

4. What are some of the possible causes for mob violence?

Reading Other Sources

Bontemps, Arna, *Chariot in the Sky: A Story of the Jubilee Singers*, New York: Winston, 1951.

Brown, Claude, *Manchild in the Promised Land*, New York: Macmillan, 1965.

Griffin, John Howard, *Black Like Me*, Boston: Houghton Mifflin, 1960.

Kytle, Elizabeth, *Willie Mae: The Life of a Negro Servant in the Deep South*, New York: Signet, 1964.

Meltzer, Milton and Meier, August, *Time of Trial, Time of Hope: The Negro in America, 1919-1941*, Garden City, New York: Doubleday, 1966.

Sterling, Dorothy, *Mary Jane*, Garden City, New York: Doubleday, 1959.

Tarry, Ellen, *The Third Door*, New York: McKay, 1955.

Washington, Booker T., *Up From Slavery*, New York: Bantam, 1963.

White, William L., *Lost Boundaries*, New York: Harcourt, 1948.

Wright, Richard, *Uncle Tom's Children*, New York: Signet, 1963.

5. The Civil Rights Movement

We shall overcome,
We shall overcome,
We shall overcome someday,
Deep in my heart,
I do believe,
We shall overcome someday.

We Shall Overcome

Why was the Civil Rights Movement organized?

One method for people to accomplish their goals is to band together in an organization. More will be accomplished if people will join together rather than working separately. American Negroes and whites have banded together in civil rights organizations to work for the civil rights of Negroes. The goals of the civil rights organizations are the full rights, duties, and rewards of citizenship for the American Negro.

What are some of the civil rights organizations?

The oldest civil rights organizations are the National Association for the Advancement of Colored People (NAACP) and the National Urban League. The NAACP was founded in 1909, and the National Urban League was founded in 1910. The National Association for the Advancement of Colored People was formed out of an earlier organization called the Niagara Movement. William Edward Burghart DuBois helped start the Niagara Movement in 1905. He called together a small group of Negro leaders to meet in Buffalo, New York. These leaders decided to protest against segregation and to win civil rights for American Negroes. Four years later, the leaders of the Niagara Movement joined with a few other Negroes and whites to form the National Association for the Advancement of Colored People. The main goals of the NAACP were to protect Negro voting rights, to end lynching, to gain better educational opportunities for Negroes, and to destroy segregation.

The main goal of the National Urban League has been to help Negro migrants adjust to the ways of living in a large city. Life in the large cities was confusing and frightening to Negroes who were accustomed to living on farms or in small towns. These migrants needed help in finding a job and a decent place to live. They needed protection against the people in the cities who would try to cheat them. They needed help in overcoming prejudice and discrimination. The leaders of the National Urban League were determined to meet these needs of Negro migrants to the large northern cities of the United States. This migration of southern Negroes to northern cities was one of the largest movements of people in the history of the United States of America.

Other important civil rights organizations are the Congress of Racial Equality (CORE), the Southern Christian Leadership Conference (SCLC), and the Student Non-Violent Coordinating Committee (SNCC). These organizations were also formed to fight for civil rights and to end segregation.

Reverend Martin Luther King, Jr. founded the SCLC in 1956.

The Southern Christian Leadership Conference is today one of the larger and more famous civil rights groups in America. Reverend King has called segregation a disgrace to all Americans. He has asked for all Americans to help destroy segregation.

How have civil rights organizations tried to end segregation and gain civil rights for Negroes?

Each of the civil rights organizations has its own favorite method for fighting segregation. The NAACP has relied on the law and the Supreme Court as its method to end segregation. In most cases the NAACP has succeeded. The year of the NAACP's first big success was 1915. The NAACP appealed to the Supreme Court to do away with grandfather clauses for voting. The NAACP said these laws were unconstitutional because they violated the Fifteenth Amendment. Another victory came in 1917 when the Supreme Court overthrew a Louisiana law that required Negroes to live in a certain area or section of a city.

The greatest victory of the NAACP was won in 1954. The United States Supreme Court decided that segregation in public schools must be ended. This decision overthrew the "separate but equal" decision in the *Plessy vs. Ferguson* case of 1896. Justice Earl Warren said that is was impossible to have separate but equal schools for Negroes.

He argued that separate Negro schools were always inferior. Forcing Negroes to attend separate schools made Negroes think of themselves as inferior to whites. It made Negroes think that they were not good enough to be educated with white students. Justice Earl Warren said that segregated schools deprived Negro children of an equal education.

In 1963 an unsuccessful attempt was made by the governor of Alabama, George Wallace, to bar Negro students from entering the University of Alabama.

Army troops kept a protective watch when nine Negro students entered Central High School in Little Rock, Arkansas.

Since the *Brown vs. the Board of Education* decision in 1954, schools in the South have been slowly *integrating*. Integration is the end of the practices of segregation. But integration has not been accomplished easily in the South. Many white leaders have criticized the Supreme Court for its decision in this case. These white leaders have tried to resist school integration by not obeying the Supreme Court decision. The NAACP has continued to appeal to the United States courts and to the President to force southern states to end school segregation. President Dwight Eisenhower sent the United States Army to Little Rock, Arkansas in 1957 to protect nine Negro students who were attempting to attend Central High School.

These Negro teenagers entered Central High School during the early days of September, 1957. Mobs of white adults stood outside the school and yelled insults at the nine Negro students. The Negro students were afraid of mob violence and withdrew from the school. Federal soldiers were sent to Little Rock by President Eisenhower on September 25. The soldiers were to escort the nine students to and from school and to protect them from danger. Gradually people were convinced to allow the nine Negroes to attend Central High School in peace.

What other events helped force school integration?

President John F. Kennedy sent federal law officers to Oxford, Mississippi in 1962. These federal officials were sent to force the University of Mississippi to allow a Negro to go to school there. The University of Mississippi was a segregated school, and officials did not want to admit any Negroes. James Meredith, a Negro, wanted to attend the University of Mississippi.

James Meredith was qualified in every way to attend the university, and he insisted upon his right under the law to attend the University of Mississippi. Meredith was accompanied by several federal officials when he came to Oxford, Mississippi. A crowd of white people gathered and a riot took place. One white reporter was killed, and several other people were injured. Meredith attended the university, and later he graduated from the university.

The federal government has put pressure on the states that have been slowest in ending segregation in their schools. As a result of this federal action, the five states of Alabama, Georgia, Louisiana, Mississippi, and South Carolina had about 10,000 Negroes in integrated schools in 1965. In 1964, there were only 2,000 Negroes in integrated schools in these five states. It is a very slow process, but it seems as though segregation in the public schools of the United States will be ended in the future.

What methods have been used by other civil rights groups?

The National Urban League has been active in civil rights by helping Negroes to find jobs, to find decent homes, and to become accustomed to life in the city. The Urban League has also influenced state and local governments to pass laws for the protection of Negro rights.

One of the main successes of the Urban League has been the passage of *fair employment practices laws* in many states and cities. These laws protect Negroes against unfair treatment when they try to get jobs. They also protect Negroes against being cheated out of fair wages or job promotions. Seventeen states and several cities around the United States have passed fair employment practices laws since 1945.

James Meredith was the first Negro to integrate the University of Mississippi.

When Stokely Carmichael was head of the Student Non-Violent Coordinating Committee, he advocated more radical methods to gain civil rights for Afro-Americans.

The Congress of Racial Equality, the Student Non-Violent Coordinating Committee, and the Southern Christian Leadership Conference have emphasized non-violent mass protests and public demonstrations as their main method of ending segregation and gaining civil rights. These methods were first used successfully by Reverend Martin Luther King, Jr. in Montgomery, Alabama. In 1955 Mrs. Rosa Parks, a Negro, boarded a bus and took a seat near the back of the bus. This section at the rear of the bus was reserved for Negroes. The bus picked up more passengers, and soon all the seats on the bus were filled. When four more white people got on the bus, the driver ordered Mrs. Parkes and three other Negroes to give their seats to the white people. Mrs. Parkes said,

"No!" Her refusal was a crime in the segregated city of Montgomery, and she was arrested. Negro citizens of Montgomery decided to protest this arrest by *boycotting* the bus company. This meant they refused to ride the buses in the city of Montgomery. The Negroes walked, hitched rides, formed auto pools, or drove everywhere they went. The boycott lasted for 382 days. One of the leaders of the boycott was Reverend King who was only twenty-six years old. The bus boycott ended when the United States Supreme Court overthrew the Alabama law that required segregation on the buses. King and his followers had won a striking victory against segregation by the use of peaceful means of public protest and non-violent demonstration. Non-violent protest was successful.

Freedom riders often faced danger from white mobs. This bus was burned when a mob threw a fire bomb through the window near Anniston, Alabama.

The peaceful methods of Reverend King were followed by other Negro leaders. In Greensboro, North Carolina in February, 1960, Negro college students tried to get service at a segregated lunch counter. When they were refused service, they remained seated so that no one else could be served. This type of demonstration was called a *sit-in*. These demonstrations soon spread to other cities as a means to end segregated public facilities such as restaurants, cafeterias, and beaches. Almost all of these sit-in demonstrations were non - violent. Even when white people insulted or attacked the demonstrators, the demonstrators would not fight back. Many demonstrators were arrested and were forced to spend time in jail or to pay fines. But sit-in demonstrations were successful in ending segregated lunch counters and restaurants.

In 1961 and 1962 the Congress of Racial Equality used a new non-violent demonstration method called the *freedom ride*. Demonstrators would board buses and trains and would refuse to sit in the seats reserved for Negroes only. At bus, train, and airline stations they demanded to use waiting rooms, washrooms, and lunch counters. These freedom riders were insulted and attacked by white segregationists and were arrested by the police. But finally the law ruled in favor of the freedom riders. Transportation facilities all over the South slowly began to be integrated.

What were the Birmingham demonstrations?

The *centennial* of the Emancipation Proclamation was in 1963. This was the 100th anniversary of President Lincoln's freeing of the slaves. During 1963, Negroes wanted to draw attention to the many injustices Negroes had suffered for the past one hundred years. During the first few months of 1963, Negroes demonstrated for civil rights in several cities in the South.

These demonstrations reached a high point in Birmingham, Alabama. Reverend King had called Birmingham the most segregated city in the United States. He pointed out that while 40 percent of Birmingham's population was Negro, only 8 percent of these Negroes were registered to vote. King promised to lead demonstrations in Birmingham until segregation there was completely destroyed. Birmingham Negroes marched almost every day under the leadership of Reverend King. They carried signs demanding civil rights. They also sang freedom songs such as *We Shall Overcome*. Reverend King told his followers again and again that these demonstrations must be non-violent. He said this non-violent protest was the only way to protest. If violence happened, it would be done by the white people in Birmingham. No violence would be committed by the Negro citizens of Birmingham.

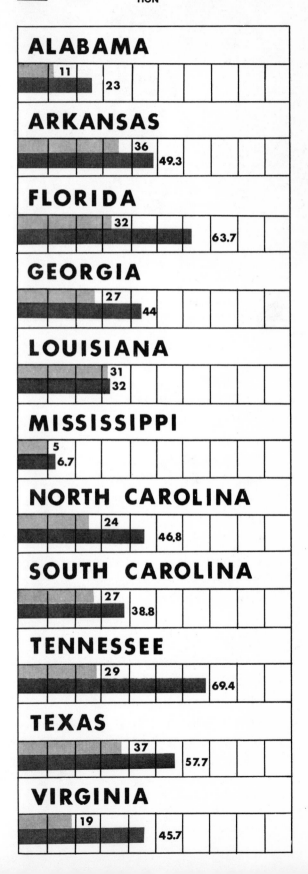

NEGRO VOTER REGISTRATION

1956
1964

NUMBERS INDICATE PERCENTAGE OF TOTAL VOTING AGE POPULATION

ALABAMA
11
23

ARKANSAS
36
49.3

FLORIDA
32
63.7

GEORGIA
27
44

LOUISIANA
31
32

MISSISSIPPI
5
6.7

NORTH CAROLINA
24
46.8

SOUTH CAROLINA
27
38.8

TENNESSEE
29
69.4

TEXAS
37
57.7

VIRGINIA
19
45.7

Many people have complained about the use of police dogs, guns, and fire hoses by the police to stop civil rights demonstrations.

bama Governor George Wallace sent hundreds of state troopers to stop the riots. Demonstrations in Birmingham were ended in May. Reverend King and his followers won a few small gains from the city officials. The main achievement of the demonstrations was to draw the attention of the nation to the conditions in Birmingham and therefore to other cities in the South.

Throughout the rest of the summer of 1963, mass protest demonstrations were held in most of the cities of the South and in a few northern cities. The *Civil Rights Revolution* had started. The Civil Rights Revolution is the name some people gave to this drive for civil rights during the 1960's.

What happened during the demonstrations in Birmingham?

The Birmingham police treated the demonstrators harshly. They used fire hoses and police dogs to stop the demonstrations. Many marchers were arrested until the jails were overflowing. Reverend King was one of the demonstrators arrested. White leaders finally agreed to cooperate with the Negro demonstrators to end segregation of some public facilities. Reverend King agreed to end the protest demonstrations.

This agreement between white and Negro leaders ended on May 11, 1963 when the headquarters of the Southern Christian Leadership Conference was bombed. Angry Negroes rioted in protest against these bombings. Ala-

Martin Luther King, Jr. continued his leadership of civil rights demonstrations in northern cities until his murder in April, 1968.

What was the March on Washington?

The largest protest demonstration for civil rights was the March on Washington. This demonstration took place on August 28, 1963. Over 200,000 people came from all areas of the United States to take part in the protest march. Many of the demonstrators were white people who wanted to show their support for the Civil Rights Movement. The march was planned and led by the various civil rights organizations. Its purpose was to inform Congress and the people of the United States that Negroes expected and wanted a civil rights law to be passed. The demonstrators demanded that the federal government act to help destroy segregation. *Freedom Now* and *We Shall Overcome* were the slogans of the March on Washington. As a result, the Civil Rights Act became law in 1964.

What violence has occurred during the Civil Rights Revolution?

Terrible violence shook the United States during the summer of 1963. Although Reverend King and many other civil rights leaders emphasized non-violence, violence was a part of that long, hot summer of civil rights protest and demonstration.

Medgar Evers, a NAACP leader, was shot and killed as he walked toward the door of his home in Jackson, Mississippi. Four young Negro girls were killed when a bomb exploded in the 16th Street Baptist Church in Birmingham, Alabama. A short time later two Negro boys were shot and killed on the streets of Birmingham, Alabama.

Violence also occurred during the summer of 1964. Negroes rioted in Harlem. Property was destroyed and hundreds of people were injured.

The March on Washington in 1963 was probably the greatest peaceful demonstration ever held in the national capital.

The volunteer workers of the 1964 Mississippi Summer Project were continually faced with violence. This project was organized by the Council of Federated Organizations (COFO) in order to help Negroes register to vote in Mississippi. Nearly 1,000 young adults from all parts of the nation volunteered to go to Mississippi as part of this project. Mississippi segregationists were angry about this project. They threatened and insulted the project workers. Andrew Goodman, Michael Schwerner, and James Chaney were murdered in Mississippi that summer for taking part in the project. Several members of the Ku Klux Klan were later arrested and found guilty of violating the Civil Rights Act.

What was the 1964 Civil Rights Act?

The hard work of all of the civil rights organizations was rewarded on June 19, 1964, when Congress passed the 1964 Civil Rights Act. This law was a great step forward in the Negro struggle for equal rights. This law said hotels, motels, restaurants, theaters, and sports arenas cannot discriminate against Negroes. These public facilities cannot refuse to serve them, and they cannot make Negroes sit or use separate facilities. Segregation in parks, playgrounds, and swimming pools also was ended. The law also stated that the same voter qualification standards must be applied to both whites and Negroes. There must be no difference in registration or voting requirements for citizens.

Michael Schwerner, left, James Chaney, middle, and Andrew Goodman, right, were three civil rights workers murdered during the summer of 1964 near Philadelphia, Mississippi.

President Lyndon B. Johnson signs the 1964 Civil Rights Act into law. This was the first major civil rights legislation since 1875.

The law stated that literacy tests can no longer be used unfairly in order to keep Negroes from voting. The Civil Rights Act stops discrimination in hiring Negroes and the payment of different wages to Negroes and whites. Companies with one hundred or more workers can no longer hire only white people. No longer can these companies pay better wages to white people than to Negroes who do the same job. The federal government is given the power to withhold funds from any state where racial discrimination is practiced in public education and health programs.

What people were dissatisfied with the Civil Rights Act?

Some people have bitterly criticized the Civil Rights Act. Segregationists have been disgusted with the law because it strikes at the heart of their beliefs about race. Other people have said that the Civil Rights Act gives too much power to the federal gov-ernment. These people think it is wrong for the federal government to be able to tell a hotel owner or a res-taurant owner who can be served. These people believe that owning a business is a private matter, and the government should stay out of pri-vate business.

Even though the Civil Rights Act was passed in 1964, many Negroes were not completely satisfied. They continued to demonstrate and to pro-test for complete civil rights equality. Certain civil rights were still witheld from them. The most famous protest demonstration of 1965 was in Ala-bama. More than half the people of Selma, Alabama were Negroes. Yet 99 percent of the voters of Selma were white. Nearly all of the Negroes of Selma were kept from voting. Rever-end King said this inequality of vot-ing rights was wrong. He decided to draw the attention of the nation to this unfair treatment of Negroes in Selma and other southern cities.

113

A huge march from Selma to Montgomery, the state capital, was planned. Governor George Wallace ordered the state troopers to halt the march. The night of March 9, three white clergymen were beaten by white segregationists. One of them, Reverend James J. Reeb, was beaten so badly that he died. At this time the federal government stepped in and ordered the state government of Alabama not to interfere with the civil rights marchers. President Lyndon B. Johnson sent United States Army troops and Federal Bureau of Investigation (FBI) agents to Alabama to protect the marchers. On March 21, the march from Selma to Montgomery began. Twenty - five thousand Negroes and whites joined this march. The march was led by Reverend King. When the marchers reached the state capital of Montgomery, Reverend King made a speech saying that segregation was wrong. He said that his followers would never rest until segregation was ended. He called upon the state government of Alabama to protect the voting rights of its Negro citizens. Another tragedy soon followed. Mrs. Viola Gregg Liuzzo, a white civil rights worker from Detroit, Michigan, was murdered. She was shot while driving some demonstrators back to Selma after the protest march to Montgomery. No one was ever caught or convicted of this murder of Mrs. Liuzzo.

What happened to cause the riot in Los Angeles in the summer of 1965?

Racial violence occurred in several cities during the summer of 1965. The worst violence, however, was in the city of Los Angeles. On the evening of August 11, a Negro youth was arrested for drunken driving. The young man resisted arrest by the police. The police used force to arrest him. A crowd of Negroes gathered, and they became angry at the police for using force. Rumors spread that the police had brutally beaten another young man and his mother. Negro youths began to throw rocks and bottles at the police. Soon a large riot was taking place. This wild riot lasted for five long days.

What was the result of the riot in Los Angeles?

Negro rioters smashed store windows and carried out furniture, clothes, food, appliances, and liquor. They burned buildings and hurled stones at the police. They shot bullets at firemen who were trying to put out the fires. They beat any white people who traveled into the area, and they attacked the police with stones, bottles, bricks, and guns. It was necessary for the governor of the state of California to call out the national guard to restore order to the city. The riot caused thirty-four deaths. Almost nine hundred people were injured. Over 4,000 people were arrested. There were 209 buildings destroyed by fire and 787 other buildings were damaged. There was about $46 million worth of property losses. As in all race riots, people were killed or injured who had nothing to do with causing the riot. The result was increased misery and suffering for both the Negroes and whites who lived in Los Angeles.

What are the causes of racial violence in the cities?

Most people have wondered about the causes of riots in the large cities of the United States. Some people have blamed the riots entirely on hoodlums and gangsters. Other people have said the riots are caused because Negroes are not satisfied with the opportunities available to them.

Some people have said the riots were caused because all Negroes behave this way. All people should understand that misery, poverty, and unequal treatment of Negroes have caused many Negroes to look for an escape from poverty and discrimination. The miserable living conditions in the ghetto have caused some Negroes to act desperately in order to try and improve themselves. Many public officials have recognized this problem and have called for federal action to eliminate poverty and misery. If the poverty and misery is eliminated, some of the causes of the riots will be eliminated. If voting rights and equal opportunities are given to Negroes, other causes of the riots will be eliminated.

A taxi overturned in the streets of Los Angeles shows the violence during the Los Angeles riots in 1965.

Violence continues in the cities. National Guard troops were called into Detroit in the summer of 1967.

What is the Voting Rights Act?

The largest success of the Civil Rights Movement in 1965 was the passing of the Voting Rights Act by Congress. The purpose of this law is to protect Negro voting rights. It ends unfair literacy tests as a requirement for voting. The law allows the use of federal examiners to register Negroes in areas where local officials will not register these people to vote. It was expected that this Voting Rights Act would add over one million new Negro voters in the various southern states.

What civil rights demonstrations occurred in 1966?

Protests and demonstrations for Negro civil rights continued in 1966. James Meredith began a protest march across the entire state of Mississippi in order to encourage Negroes to register to vote. A few days after the march began, Meredith was shot from ambush by a white man. James Meredith recovered after a few days in the hospital. His protest march was continued by Reverend King and other civil rights leaders. In Grenada, Mississippi, the Southern Christian Leadership Conference held daily demonstrations to protest the resistance of Mississippi white people against Negro civil rights.

The largest civil rights demonstrations came in cities outside the South. Martin Luther King, Jr. said that it was time to draw attention to the problems of the Negro ghettos in large northern cities, such as Chicago, Detroit, New York, and Cleveland. Reverend King criticized these cities for forcing Negroes to live in ghettos. He called for *open occupancy laws* which would give Negroes the right to buy homes or rent apartments in any section of the city. Negroes would no longer be forced to live in the ghetto.

Chicago was selected as the place to begin demonstrations for open occupancy laws. Reverend King joined with several Chicago civil rights leaders to help organize protest marches into some of the all-white neighborhoods of Chicago. During July and August several protest marches were held each week. Usually the marchers were met with insults and rocks thrown by white bystanders. Reverend King was hit and injured by one of these rocks. Chicago police worked hard to protect the marchers. They arrested many whites who were trying to start racial trouble.

WITHERING HEIGHTS

Many white people were against the open occupancy laws. These people feared that the value of their property would go down if Negroes moved into the neighborhood. They pointed out that most Negroes live in run-down neighborhoods. They said the same thing would happen to their neighborhoods if Negroes were allowed to move there. Some white people were against the open occupancy laws because they believed the government should not have the power to tell property owners to whom they could rent or sell. And some white people were against the open occupancy laws because they believed in segregation and the racist ideas about the behavior of Negroes.

117

Reverend King called off the open occupancy demonstrations after Chicago officials promised to take steps to give better housing opportunities to Negroes. Negro leaders hoped this would help end the ghettos in Chicago and other large cities.

The methods that Negroes have used to change their status are part of the great American tradition of organizing and fighting for freedom and equality. Like the patriots of the 1770's, American Negroes of the 1960's have protested against unfair treatment. The Negro "civil rights revolution" has been for the most part peaceful and lawful. This right to assemble and peacefully demonstrate is guaranteed by the United States Constitution.

How has the Civil Rights Movement affected the progress of Afro-Americans?

The Civil Rights Movement has improved the status and the role of Negroes in American life. Today, Negroes have a better chance for an education, a good job, good wages, and a good life. More and more Negroes are taking leadership roles in government, education, and business. Negroes have been freed from the insult of being refused service at restaurants or hotels. The status of all Negroes has been improved with the breakdown of the segregation system.

American Negroes have made their greatest progress in education. In 1870 only about one out of every twenty Negroes could read and write. Only a handful of Negroes had completed any higher education. Today almost all adult American Negroes can read and write. Every year over 10,000 Negroes graduate from American colleges and universities.

There have also been great gains in job opportunities. In 1940 only 17 percent of all Negro men worked at semi-skilled or skilled jobs. In 1940 only 2 percent of all Negroes worked in professional or technical occupations such as doctors, lawyers, professors and engineers. By 1964 almost 7 percent of all Negroes worked in professional or technical occupations. In 1939 the median male Negro income was $460 per year. This was about 41 percent of the white male median income of $1,112. By 1966 the median income for a Negro male was $4,600 per year, which was about 60 percent of the median income of $7,700 for a white male in the U.S. In 1966, 30 percent of families in the United States with incomes over $7,000 per year were Negro families.

Life expectancy for Negroes has increased greatly. In 1900 the death rate for Negroes was twenty-five per every thousand Negro people. In 1900 the death rate for whites was seventeen per every thousand white people. In 1960 the death rate for Negroes and whites was almost the same. This rate was about ten people per thousand. These figures show that Negroes have been able to receive better medical care and to have better diets.

The Civil Rights Movement has caused Negroes to take more pride in themselves and their race. The victories of the Civil Rights Movement were won by Negroes for Negroes. These victories were not gained easily. They were won through hard work and great skill and tremendous patience. The successes of the Civil Rights Movement have caused many whites to have greater respect for Negroes, and many Negroes to have greater respect for themselves.

Poiner in The Detroit

"What do I have to lose?"

"We Ain't Prejudiced..."

Senseless Antagonists

THE NIAGARA MOVEMENT

In June, 1905, the Niagara Movement was started by a group of Negro leaders. This was the beginning of the twentieth century drive for civil rights. The National Association for the Advancement of Colored People grew out of the Niagara Movement. W. E. B. DuBois was one of the founders of the Niagara Movement. DuBois explains the purpose of the movement in this document.

The Niagara Movement is an organization composed at present of 54 men resident in 18 states of the United States. These men . . . have banded themselves together into an organization. This organization was perfected at a meeting held at Buffalo, New York, 1905 and was called "The Niagara Movement. . . ."

What now are the principles upon which the membership of the Niagara Movement are agreed? As set forth briefly in the constitution, they are as follows:

a) Freedom of speech and criticism.
b) An unfettered and unsubsidized press.
c) Manhood suffrage.
d) The abolition of all caste distinctions based simply on race and color.
e) The recognition of the principle of human brotherhood as a practical present creed.
f) The recognition of the highest and best training as the monopoly of no class or race.
g) A belief in the dignity of labor.
h) United effort to realize these ideals under wise and courageous leadership.

All of these things we believe are of great and instant importance; there has been a determined effort in this country to stop the free expression of opinion among black men . . . the principles of democratic government are losing ground, and caste distinctions are growing in all directions. Human brotherhood is spoken of today with a smile and a sneer, effort is being made to curtail the educational opportunities of the colored children. . . . If we expect to gain our rights . . . then . . . we must complain. Yes, plain, blunt complaint, ceaseless agitation, unfailing exposure of dishonesty and wrong—this is the ancient, unerring way to liberty, and we must follow it. . . . These are the things that we as black men must try to do.

To press the matter of stopping the curtailment of our political rights.

To urge Negroes to vote intelligently and effectively.

To push the matter of civil rights.

To organize business co-operation.

To build school houses and increase the interest in education.

To open up new avenues of employment and strengthen our hold on the old.

To distribute tracts and information in regard to the laws of health.

To bring Negroes and labor unions into mutual understanding.

To study Negro history.

To increase the circulation of honest, unsubsidized newspapers and periodicals.

To attack crime among us by all civilized agencies. In fact to do all in our power by word or deed to increase the efficiency of our race, the enjoyment of its manhood rights, and the performance of its just duties.

This is a large program. It cannot be realized in a short time. But something can be done and we are going to do something. . . . Are we not men enough to protest . . . and dare to stand up and be counted as demanding every single right that belongs to free American citizens? This is the critical time, Black men of America; the staggering days of emancipation, of childhood are gone.

SEPARATE MEANS UNEQUAL

In 1954 the United States Supreme Court overturned the "separate but equal" decision made by the Supreme Court in 1896 in the *Plessy vs. Ferguson* case. In this case, *Brown vs. Board of Education, Topeka, Kansas*, the Supreme Court said that Negroes must not be forced to go to segregated public schools. The reason was that these schools were not equal to the schools for white children. Mr. Chief Justice Earl Warren gave the unanimous opinion of the Supreme Court on May 17, 1954.

. . . minors of the Negro race, through their legal representatives, seek the aid of the courts in obtaining admission to the public schools of their community on a nonsegregated basis. In each instance, they had been denied admission to schools attended by white children under laws requiring or permitting segregation according to race. This segregation was alleged to deprive the the plaintiffs of the equal protection of the laws under the Fourteenth Amendment. . . .

The plaintiffs contend that segregated public schools are not "equal" and cannot be made "equal," and that hence they are deprived of the equal protection of the laws. . . .

In approaching this problem, we cannot turn the clock back to 1868 when the Amendment was adopted, or even to 1896 when *Plessy v. Ferguson* was written. We must consider public education in the light of its full development and its present place in American life throughout the Nation. Only in this way can it be determined if segregation in public schools deprives these plaintiffs of the equal protection of the laws.

Today, education is perhaps the most important function of state and local governments. Compulsory school attendance laws and the great expenditures for education both demonstrate our recognition of the importance of education to democratic society. It is required in the performance of our most basic public responsibilities, even service in the armed forces. It is the very foundation of good citizenship. Today it is a principal instrument in awakening the child to cultural values, in preparing him for later professional training, and in helping him to adjust normally to his environment. In these days, it is doubtful that any child may reasonably be expected to succeed in life if he is denied the opportunity of an education. Such an opportunity where the state has undertaken to provide it, is a right which must be made available to all on equal terms.

We come then to the question presented: Does segregation of children in public schools solely on the basis of race, even though the physical facilities and other "tangible" factors may be equal, deprive the children of the minority group of equal educational opportunities? We believe that it does. . . .

To separate them from others of similar age and qualifications solely because of their race generates a feeling of inferiority as to their status in the community that may affect their hearts and minds in a way unlikely ever to be undone. . . .

We conclude that in the field of public education the doctrine of "separate but equal" has no place. Separate educational facilities are inherently unequal. Therefore, we hold that the plaintiffs . . . are . . . deprived of the equal protection of the laws guaranteed by the Fourteenth Amendment.

CONFLICT IN THE SOUTH

Robert Penn Warren is a famous white writer from the South. He was born in Kentucky in 1905 and has been a teacher at several southern universities. His most famous book is *All the King's Men*. In 1956 Warren traveled through five southern states to talk to all kinds of people about segregation and integration of the white and Negro people. This document tells about these travels and these conversations.

I was going back to look at the landscapes and streets I had known—Kentucky, Tennessee, Arkansas, Mississippi, Louisiana—to look at the faces, to hear the voices, to hear, in fact, the voices in my own blood. A girl from Mississippi had said to me: "I feel it's all happening inside of me, every bit of it. It's all there." I know what she meant. . . .

The man in the seat beside me on the plane is offering me a newspaper. . . . I look at the man. He is a big man, very big, bulging over the seat, bulging inside his blue serge. He is fiftyish, hair graying. His face is large and raw-looking, heavy-jowled, thick gray eyebrows over small, deep-set appraising eyes. . . .

I began to read the paper, an article about the riots at the University of Alabama. He notices what I am reading. "Bet you thought I was from down there." he said. "From the way I talk. But I ain't. I was born and raised in New York City, but I been in the scrap business down here ten years. Didn't you think I was from down here?"

"Yes," I say, for that seems the sociable thing to say.

He twists his bulk in the blue serge and reaches and stabs a finger at the headline about Alabama. "Folks could be more gen'rous and fair-thinking," he says. "Like affable, you might say, and things would work out. If folks get affable and contig'ous, you might say, things sort of get worked out in time, but you get folks not being affable-like and stirring things up and it won't work out. Folks on both sides the question."

He asks me if I don't agree, and I say, sure, I agree. Sure, if folks were just affable-like.

I am thinking of what a taxi driver had said to me in Memphis: "Looks like the Lucy girl wouldn't want to go no place where people throwed eggs at her and sich. But if they's jist let her alone, them Goodrich plant fellers and all, it would blow over. What few niggers come would not have stayed no duration. Not when they found she couldn't git the social stuff, and all. . . ."

And a taxi driver in Nashville, a back-country man come to the city, a hard, lean, spare face, his lean shoulders humped forward over the wheel so that the clavicles show through the coat: "A black-type person and a white-type person, they ain't alike. Now the black-type person, all they think about is fighting and having a good time and you know that. Now the white-type person is more American-type, he don't mind fighting but he don't fight to kill for fun. It's that cannibal blood you caint get out."

Now, on the plane, my companion observes me scribbling something in a notebook.

"You a writer or something?" he asks. "A newspaper fellow, maybe?"

I say yes.

"You interested in that stuff?" he asks, and points to the article. "Somebody ought to tell 'em not to blame no state, not even Alabam' or Mississippi, for what the bad folks do. Like stuff in New York or Chicago. Folks in Mississippi got good hearts as any. They always been nice and good-hearted to me, for I go up to a man affable. The folks down here is just in trouble and can't claw out. Don't blame 'em, got good hearts but can't claw out of their trouble. It is hard to claw out from under the past and the past way."

He asks me if I have been talking to a lot of people.

I had been talking to a lot of people. . . .

Just listening to talk as it comes is best, but sometimes it doesn't come, or the man says, "You ask me some questions," and so, bit by bit, a certain pattern of questions emerges, the old obvious questions, I suppose—the questions people respond to or flinch from.

What are the white man's reasons for segregation?

. . . a very black man, small-built and intense, leans forward in his chair. He says it is money, so that the white man can have cheap labor, can make money. . . .

Later, I am talking with the hill-man organizer . . . and he is telling me why he wants segregation. "The Court," he says, "hit caint take no stick and mix folks up like you swivel and swull eggs broke in a bowl. Naw," he says, "you got to raise 'em up, the niggers, not bring the white folks down to nigger level." He illustrates with his pudgy, strong hands in the air before him, one up, one down, changing levels. . . .

Then I talk with a Negro grade-school teacher, in the country, in Tennessee. . . . She is sitting in her tiny, pridefully clean house, with a prideful bookcase of books beyond her, talking with slow and detached tones. . . . I ask her why white people want to keep segregation.

"You ought to see the school house I teach in," she says, and her lips curl sardonically, "set in the mud and hogs can come under it, and the privies set back in the mud. And see some of the children that come there, out of homes with nothing, worse than the school house, no sanitation or cleanness, with disease and dirt and no manners. You wouldn't blame a white person for not wanting the white child set down beside them." Then with a slow movement of the shoulders, again the curl of the lips: "Why didn't the Federal Government give us money ten years ago for our school? To get us ready, to raise us up a little to integrate. It would have made it easier. . . ."

I am talking with an official of one of those segregation outfits, late at night, in his house, in a fringe subdivision, in a small living room. . . . My host is seventy-five years old, bald except for a fringe of gray hair, sallow-skinned, very clean and scrubbed-looking, white shirt but no tie, a knife-edge crease to his hard finish gray trousers. . . .

I ask him why the white man wants segregation.

"He'll say one thing and another," he says, "he knows in his bones it ain's right to have mixing. But you got to give him the reasons, explain it to him. . . . You got to explain how no Negroes . . . ever created a civilization. They are parasites. They haven't got the stuff up here." And he taps his forehead. . . .

Now and then, I encounter a man whose argument for segregation, in the present context, has nothing to do with the Negro at all. At its simplest level its spokesman says: "I don't give a durn about the niggers, they never bother me one way or another. But I don't like being forced. Ain't no man ever forced me."

But the law always carries force, you say.

"Not this law. It's different. It ain't our law. . . ."

And I hear a college student in the Deep South: "You know, it's just that people don't like to feel like they're spitting on their grandfather's grave. They feel some connection they don't want to break. Something would bother them if they broke it."

The young man is, I gather, an integrationist. He adds: "And sometimes something bothers them if they don't break it."

LETTERS FROM MISSISSIPPI

During the summer of 1964, nearly 1,000 young white adults visited Mississippi as part of the Mississippi Summer Project. This project was organized by the leading Negro civil rights organizations. The purpose was to help Mississippi Negroes to register to vote, to organize for political action, to set-up "Freedom Schools" to teach about civil rights and Negro history, and to help end segregation. Many of the white volunteers wrote letters home to their parents and friends telling about their experiences.

Canvassing, the main technique in voter registration, is an art. . . .

Techniques and approaches vary. Mine is often like this: Hi. My name is Steve M. (shake hands, having gotten his name, address, from a mailbox). I'm with COFO. There are a lot of us working in this area, going from house to house trying to encourage people to go down and register to vote. (Pause) Are you a registered voter? (This is the direct techniques. Often people, being afraid, will lie and say yes, but you can usually tell, because they will be very proud.) Are you planning on going down soon? (This makes them declare themselves). Usually they say "yes" or "I hadn't thought much about it." The other answer is "No, I ain't going down at all." "Well, I have a sample of the registration form." (Take it out and hand it to them.) "You know, some people are a little afraid to go down because they don't quite know what they're getting into. It's something new and different, and they're not sure about it."

Then I go on, "You know, it is so important that everyone gets to vote. As it stands now, that man downtown in charge of roads doesn't have to listen to Negroes. They can't put him out of office. He should be working for you." (Much gossip, chatter, mutual questions through all this). . . .

You get the picture. It goes on, 10 hours a day, 6 days a week.

We're all a little nervous. Four COFO workers—including me—are staying with the Robert Miles' on their farm just outside of Baresville. Mrs. Miles' 25 year old son Robert, Jr. is stationed out in the yard with a gun. (Yes, the Movement is still non-violent; but every farmer—white and black—in the Delta has a gun. Mr. Miles has seven, all loaded.)

Things are getting very tense around here. Last night, while I was eating a peanut butter sandwich in the kitchen and talking to the other white girl staying there, two shots whizzed right by the kitchen window—I could even see a flash of light from the gun.

Since last Saturday night when the Miles' house was bombed with a tear gas grenade, several other Negroes in town have received bomb threats. . . .

We think that the heightened tension is pretty much a testimonial to the success of our voter registration drive. About 500 Negroes have registered since the summer volunteers arrived in Batesville—this in a county where until recently only two Negroes had been able to register in seventy years.

The atmosphere in class is unbelievable. It is what every teacher dreams about—real, honest enthusiasm and desire to learn anything and everything. The girls come to class of their own free will. They respond to everything that is said. They are excited about learning. They drain me of everything that I have to offer so that I go home at night completely exhausted but very happy. . . .

I start out at 10:30 teaching . . . to about fifteen girls ranging from 15 to 25 years of age. . . . They can, for the most part, express themselves on paper but their skills in no way compare with juniors and seniors in northern suburban schools. . . .

Every class is beautiful. The girls respond, respond, respond. And they disagree among themselves. . . . They are a sharp group. But they are under-educated and starved for knowledge. They know that they have been cheated and they want anything and everything that we can give them. . . .

A while before I came down I read John Griffin's *Black Like Me* and he speaks of the hate stare. . . . It's really the most terrifying and ugly thing imaginable. When it was first given to me I had a reaction that combined fear and shock. Fear because you realize the power that someone like that will use, and shock that the human face could be that way.

As I write this letter I am on the roof of our headquarters observing a sunset I cannot even begin to describe. . . . Now and at all such times I find myself possessed by a deep melancholy, a heart-rending feeling for the black and white toilers of this state; both victims to a system that they neither created nor flourish under.

There have been incidents of violence and intimidation but they hardly seem worth noting at a time like this. I only know that I must carry on this struggle that other people have died in, and that some day that system will be changed.

THE MARCH ON WASHINGTON

Thousands of Americans traveled to Washington, D.C., on August 28, 1963. They went there to take part in a gigantic civil rights demonstration. The purpose of the march was to influence Congress to pass laws to protect the civil rights of Negroes. Reverend Martin Luther King, Jr., was one of the leaders of the march. This document contains a description of the march by Reverend King.

. . . in its glittering history, Washington has never seen a spectacle of the size and grandeur that assembled there on August 28, 1963 . . . nearly 250,000 people journeyed that day to the capital, to achieve democracy in their time.

They came from almost every state in the union; they came in every form of transportation; they gave up from one to three days' pay plus the cost of transportation, which for many was a heavy financial sacrifice. . . . It was an army without guns, but not without strength. It was an army into which no one had to be drafted. It was white and Negro, and of all ages. It had adherents of every faith, members of every class, every profession, every political party, united by a single ideal. It was a fighting army, but no one could mistake that its most powerful weapon was love. . . .

Millions of white Americans, for the first time, had a clear, long look at Negroes engaged in a serious occupation. For the first time millions listened to the informed and thoughtful words of Negro spokesmen, from all walks of life. The stereotype of the Negro suffered a heavy blow. . . .

As television beamed the image of this extraordinary gathering across the border oceans, everyone who believed in man's capacity to better himself had a moment of inspiration and confidence in the future of the human race. And every dedicated American could be proud that a dynamic experience of democracy in his nation's capital had been made visible to the world.

HUBERT H. HUMPHREY SPEAKS AGAINST SEGREGATION

When Hubert H. Humphrey was a United States Senator from Minnesota, he worked to get Negro civil rights bills passed. As Vice President of the United States, he continued this work. In this document, Vice President Humphrey tells his opinions of the Civil Rights Movement.

The Civil Rights Movement of the 1950's and 1960's is sometimes referred to as the Second American Revolution. Perhaps more accurately, it may be seen as a major phase in the continuing revolution upon which the American people embarked in 1776. . . . The campaign for equal justice and opportunity for minority groups—particularly the Negro—marks the latest battle in the long struggle of this nation toward a genuine, working democracy.

The key to solving the whole range of national problems arising from racial prejudice lies in equality of education. Without educational quality there can be neither equal opportunity in employment nor real equality at the ballot box. To the man lacking an education or training to qualify for most jobs, "fair" employment practices can be hollow benefits indeed. And the right to vote is scarcely a full achievement of the franchise for those not educated to understand the importance of the ballot. In establishing equal educational opportunity, the desegregation and integration of our schools are major and indispensable steps. . . .

One great barrier . . . is a willful and persistent desire by some to keep the Negro uneducated and unskilled. It is true that the inferior educational opportunity accorded the Negro stems in part from a shortage of funds and, under such circumstances, the desire of whites to give their own children first priority. These reasons do not explain, however, the extraordinary disparity in some areas between the funds devoted to educating white children and those alloted to educating Negro children. The February, 1962, issue of *Southern School News* reports that in Mississippi, for instance, expenditures by the school districts beyond the state's minimum allotments during the school year 1960-61 were, per pupil in average daily attendance, $81.86 for whites and only $21.77 for Negroes. Such a shocking contrast can be fully explained only by recognizing a deliberate attempt on the part of some to keep the Negro uneducated, thus to assure both a cheap pool of menial labor and a passive, nonparticipating Negro electorate.

But our society cannot refuse the Negro an equal education and then refuse to employ him in a decent job on the grounds that he is untrained. We cannot . . . say we refuse to have our children associate with the Negro because of differences in behavior. Such differences as exist result from this very pattern of forcing the Negro's exclusion from the mainstream of American life. . . .

Our schools, of course, cannot carry the total burden of integrating our society and putting an end to discrimination. Neither can the courts and the executive bear the full burden of leadership. Congress must pass the legislation that will give enforcing agencies the tools they need to implement our national policy. No one who knows the structure and workings of Congress considers this an easy task. But this problem will not disappear or be solved through the mere passage of time. Positive action is needed—needed now.

THE SOUTHERN MANIFESTO

On March 2, 1956, a group of 101 Senators and Representatives from eleven southern states presented a statement to Congress that criticized the 1954 Supreme Court decision regarding school desegregation.

We regard the decision of the Supreme Court in the school cases as a clear abuse of judicial power. . . .

This unwarranted exercise of power by the Court, contrary to the Constitution, is creating chaos and confusion in the States principally affected. It is destroying the amicable relations between the white and Negro races that have been created through 90 years of patient effort by the good people of both races. It has planted hatred and suspicion where there has been heretofore friendship and understanding.

Without regard to the consent of the governed, outside agitators are threatening immediate and revolutionary changes in our public school systems. If done, this is certain to destroy the system of public education in some of the States. . . .

We pledge ourselves to use all lawful means to bring about a reversal of this decision which is contrary to the Constitution and to prevent the use of force in its implementation.

Using Historical Methods

1. What other documents have principles similar to the principles of the Niagara Movement?

2. How would each of the goals of the Niagara Movement help to bring liberty and equality to American Negroes?

3. What are the similarities between *Plessy vs. Ferguson* and *Brown vs. Board of Education?* What are the differences?

4. What are the reasons and explanations for the statement: "We regard the decision of the Supreme Court . . . as a clear abuse of judicial power. . . ."

5. What information has been given in the documents regarding the similarity between whites and Negroes in jobs, education, health, wages, and life expectancy? What differences have been stated in the documents?

6. Look at the political cartoons in this chapter. What main idea does each cartoon give?

Knowing Your Vocabulary

integration /ˌint-ə-ˈgrā-shən/
Free association of all races and the end of segregation practices. 105

fair employment practices law
/ˈfa(ə)r im-ˈplȯi-mənt ˈprak-təs-əs ˈlȯ/
Laws to protect Negroes against unfair treatment when they apply for jobs. 106

boycott /ˈbȯi-ˌkät/
The refusal by a group of people to buy certain products or to use certain services. 107

sit-in /ˈsit-in/
A group of people sitting in a place of business so that no one else can be served. It is used as a method to end segregation. 108

freedom ride /ˈfrēd-əm rīd/
Demonstrators riding buses, trains, and other public transportation facilities to end the practices of segregation. 108

centennial /sen-ˈten-ē-əl/
The anniversary one hundred years after an event. 109

Civil Rights Revolution /ˈsiv-əl rīts ˌrev-ə-ˈlü-shən/
The name given to the demonstrations for Negro civil rights during the 1960's. 110

open occupancy law /ˈō-pən ˈäk-yə-pən-sē ˈlȯ/
Laws that give every person the right to buy or rent homes in any section of a city. 116

Reading the Text

1. What other examples in American history can you give when people have banded together in an organization to accomplish certain goals?

2. What is the main method used by each of the civil rights organizations to end segregation?

3. What are some of the problems faced by migrants to the large cities of the North?

4. Why would a boycott, a sit-in, or a freedom ride help to end the practices of segregation?

5. How did the decision in *Brown vs. the Board of Education* help cause the integration of Little Rock High School and of the University of Mississippi?

6. What are some of the main provisions of the Civil Rights Act of 1964 and the Voting Rights Act of 1965?

7. What are some of the reasons why violence has played a part in the Civil Rights Revolution?

8. What is the importance of open occupancy laws and fair employment practices laws?

9. How has the role and the status of the Negro improved during the past one hundred years?

10. What progress must still be made in gaining freedom and equality for all American citizens?

Identifying Names and Places

Civil Rights Movement
Niagara Movement
National Association for the Advancement of Colored People
National Urban League
Congress of Racial Equality
Southern Christian Leadership Conference
Student Non-Violent Coordinating Committee
Reverend Martin Luther King, Jr.
Earl Warren
Brown vs. Board of Education of Topeka, Kansas

We Shall Overcome
George Wallace
Mississippi Summer Project
Mrs. Viola Liuzzo
Voting Rights Act
James Meredith
March on Washington
Hubert H. Humphrey

Debating and Discussing Ideas

1. Have a class discussion on the causes of riots and solutions to these problems.

2. What can students do to settle the problems of racial hatred and violence?

3. Arrange a debate on the topic, "Civil rights demonstrations hurt the cause of Negro rights."

4. What are common arguments for and against open occupancy laws?

Reading Other Sources

Belfrage, Sally, *Freedom Summer*, New York: Viking, 1965.

Hughes, Langston, *Fight For Freedom: The Story of the NAACP*, New York: Berkley, 1962.

Schechter, Betty, *The Peaceable Revolution*, Boston: Houghton Mifflin, 1963.

Sutherland, Elizabeth, ed., *Letters From Mississippi*, New York: Signet, 1966.

6. Great Afro-Americans

I have learned that success
is to be measured not so much
by the position
that one has reached in life
as by the obstacles which he
has overcome while trying to succeed.

Booker T. Washington
Up From Slavery

Many Afro-Americans have achieved fame and honor. Their achievements are very remarkable because they were handicapped by many injustices that were a part of their everyday life. These injustices were racial prejudice and discrimination. But these extraordinary Americans were able to overcome these difficulties. They were able to succeed because they were very talented, they worked hard, and they made many sacrifices. Their proud record of accomplishments has contributed greatly to the progress of the United States of America.

Who were some great Negroes during the time of slavery?

Slaves had almost no chance to become outstanding individuals. Free Negroes had a slightly greater chance to become outstanding. Among these free Negroes were several great men and women.

Benjamin Banneker and Phillis Wheatley were among the first great American Negroes. They were good examples of what Negroes could accomplish if they were given an opportunity. Both Banneker and Wheatley were born free, and both were well-educated from the time of childhood. Both were encouraged to develop their extraordinary talents and skills.

Benjamin Banneker was born in Maryland before the Revolutionary War. He attended a local school for both Negro and white children. In school he was a brilliant student. He was best at mathematics, science, and astronomy. These remained his favorite subjects. In 1791 Banneker wrote the first of many *almanacs*. These almanacs were books giving the days of the week, hints for better farming and business, mathematical puzzles, and astronomical happenings. These almanacs were the first scientific writing by an American Negro. Most scientists rated Banneker's almanacs equal to the almanacs written by Benjamin Franklin. Banneker also wrote about hundreds of scientific subjects, such as bees, locusts, and clocks. Because of Banneker's scientific writings, he was selected by President George Washington to help survey and plan the national capital of Washington, D.C. In addition to his scientific work, Banneker frequently spoke out against the evils of slavery. He once wrote a letter to Thomas Jefferson asking Jefferson to end slavery and to support the cause of Negro freedom.

Phillis Wheatley was the first American Negro poet. She was born in Senegal, West Africa and was brought in a slave ship to Boston in 1761. John Wheatley, a rich businessman, bought this young slave. Later he adopted her. Phillis was well educated by John Wheatley and his wife. Phillis studied hard and learned very quickly. She began to write poetry at the age of fourteen.

Her first book of poems was published in 1773. This was only twelve years after her arrival in America. Her poetry brought her world-wide fame. She did not live to enjoy this fame because she became ill and died in 1784.

James Derham, Lemuel Haynes, Joshua Bishop, Prince Hall, Absalom Jones, and Richard Allen were other outstanding Negroes who lived during the same time as Bannecker and Wheatley. Derham was the first Negro physician in America. He was born a slave in 1762 and learned medicine from his master. Derham bought his freedom and built-up a medical practice in New Orleans.

Haynes, Bishop, Jones, and Allen were leading churchmen. Haynes was the pastor of a church in New England. The congregation of this church was white. Bishop was also the minister to a white congregation in Virginia. Jones and Allen helped start the first all Negro Christian churches in America. These all Negro churches were organized because many white people would not allow Negroes to attend the same church with them.

Hall was a hero of the Revolutionary War. Because Negroes were not allowed to join white Masonic Lodges, Hall organized the first Masonic Lodge for Negroes. Hall spent the rest of his life protesting the unfair treatment under which Negroes had to live.

Phillis Wheatley won world recognition for some of her poetry. One of her famous poems was "An Elegiac Poem on the Death of Reverend George Whitefield."

Frederick Douglass, Sojourner Truth, and Harriet Tubman were outstanding among the many Negro abolitionists. Their entire lives were spent fighting against slavery and for Negro rights.

Frederick Douglass was perhaps the greatest and the most famous of the Negro abolitionists. He was born a slave in Maryland in 1818 and escaped from slavery in 1838. Soon he began to work as an abolitionist. He traveled around the country speaking and writing against slavery. Douglass gave his first speech in 1841 at an Anti-Slavery Society meeting in Nantucket, Massachusetts. He spoke about the hardships of life as a slave. His listeners were greatly impressed. William Garrison, the famous white abolitionist, followed Douglass to the speaker's platform. platform. He shouted at the audience. "Is he a man or a thing?" Then Garrison answered that only a slave owner could call such an eloquent person a thing.

Douglass had a pleasing voice and was quite handsome. All over America he influenced crowds of people against slavery. In 1845 he traveled to England to win support for the abolitionist cause. After returning to America, Douglass founded *The North Star*, famous abolitionist newspaper.

Douglass faced danger several times. Abolitionists were not popular with many Americans. These people

Frederick Douglass was perhaps the most outstanding Negro abolitionist speaker. He traveled all over the United States speaking and writing against slavery.

especially disliked Negro abolitionists. Anti-Negro mobs often attacked Douglass' meetings. Stones were frequently thrown at Douglass. His life was even threatened, and he once had to flee to Canada.

Harriet Tubman risked her life many times to go to the South to help slaves escape on the Underground Railroad.

During the Civil War, Frederick Douglass served as an advisor to President Abraham Lincoln, He influenced Lincoln to use Negro soldiers in the Union Army. Douglass himself recruited Negro regiments for the Union Army. His own two sons fought in the Union Army.

After the Civil War, Douglass became a leader in the Republican Party. He worked as the Recorder of Deeds for the District of Columbia. In 1889 he was appointed United States ambassador to the Republic of Haiti in the West Indies.

Througout his life Frederick Douglass struggled to win civil rights for Negroes. He protested against the segregation system that was beginnig to spread all over the South. The leaders of the present day civil rights organizations look back upon Frederick Douglass as one of their greatest leaders and heroes. Douglass was one of the first civil rights workers.

Harriet Tubman and Sojourner Truth were among the greatest women abolitionists. Harriet Tubman was born a slave in Maryland and escaped from slavery when she was about twenty-five years old. She became an important part of the Underground Railroad that helped slaves escape to freedom. She made nine trips to the South and helped more than three hundred slaves escape. Harriet Tubman's work was filled with danger. At one time a $40,000 reward was offered for her capture and arrest.

During the Civil War, Harriet Tubman served the Union Army as a nurse and a scout. At times she even took part in the fighting. Once in 1863 she led a Union raiding party up the Combahee River where the Union raiding party destroyed Confederate supplies worth thousands of dollars and freed almost eight hundred slaves.

Harriet was over one hundred years old when she died in 1913. Her later years were spent campaigning for civil rights and for women's rights. Her home in Auburn, New York is maintained as a memorial to her.

Sojourner Truth was a slave who was freed in 1827. Little is known about Sojourner Truth until 1843 when she decided to become an abolitionist speaker. She devoted the remainder of her life speaking for religion and against slavery. She became a spellbinding speaker and did much to influence people against the slavery system.

Who were some famous Negro inventors, scientists, and businessmen?

Norbert Rilleux was born a slave in Louisiana. His owner recognized that Rilleux had great intelligence. The owner freed Rilleux and sent him to Paris, France to be educated. Rilleux later returned to Louisiana and became an outstanding engineer. In 1846 he invented a vacuum cup that greatly improved the method of refining sugar. Rilleux's invention lowered the cost of refining sugar and provided a better quality of sugar.

Rilleux became disgusted with the poor treatment of free Negroes in the South. Rilleux was a great scientist and inventor and became wealthy and important. Yet he was often insulted and treated badly because he was a Negro. He returned to France where he could live freely and happily. He worked there as a scientist and teacher until he died in 1894.

Paul Cuffe and James Forten were famous Negro businessmen during the era of Negro slavery. Cuffe was born free in 1759 in New Bedford, Massachusetts. He became a sailor and then a ship owner. His ships carried cargo and freight all over the world. Cuffe was very successful. He wanted to make life better for the free Negroes in New Bedford, Massachusetts. He built a school for the Negro children in New Bedford and used his own money to pay the teachers. Paul Cuffe was a very wealthy man when he died in 1817.

Norbert Rilleux was one of the most famous inventors of the 19th Century. His inventions were especially important for the sugar industry.

James Forten was a free Negro from Philadelphia. He joined the United States Navy when he was fifteen and learned all about ships and sailing. Forten became the owner of a sail-making and a shipping business. Forten was a good businessman and became quite wealthy. Forten used much of his wealth to support the Abolition Movement in the United States.

Who were some of the famous Negroes from 1863 to 1900?

The end of slavery meant new opportunities for many Negroes. Many Negroes took advantage of these opportunities and became very important people. For the first time Negroes were able to enter politics and government service. B. K. Bruce, Robert Smalls, P. B. S. Pinchback, and Robert Elliott were outstanding Negro political leaders.

B. K. Bruce was elected in 1875 as a United States Senator from Mississippi. This was an important distinction for a man who had been born a slave in 1841. Bruce obtained his freedom by running away from his owner during the Civil War. He went to Ohio and there graduated from Oberlin College. Bruce left the Senate in 1881 to serve as the Registrar of the Treasury and Recorder of Deeds in Washington, D.C. Bruce also worked with the Freedman's Bureau for many years.

Robert Smalls and a few friends took the Confederate ship "Planter" out of Charleston harbor and delivered it to the Union navy. Smalls later became captain of this ship.

Robert Smalls was born a slave in 1839 in Beaufort, South Carolina. During the Civil War he escaped from his master and joined the Union Navy. His escape was a daring adventure. Smalls and some other slaves stole a Confederate ship, the *Planter*, and sailed it out of the harbor of Charleston, South Carolina. Smalls delivered the ship to the Union Navy. As a reward for taking the *Planter* from the Confederates, Smalls was made a pilot in the United States Navy. He continued to pilot the *Planter* and later was made captain of this ship.

After the Civil War, Robert Smalls entered politics. He helped write a new constitution for the state of South Carolina. He served as a representative in the South Carolina legislature from 1868 to 1874. And he was a Representative in the United States Congress from 1875 to 1887. While he was in the United States Congress, Smalls helped write the Civil Rights Act of 1875.

Pinckney Benton Stewart Pinchback was the only Negro to ever serve as the governor of a state. He had been elected lieutenant governor of the state of Louisiana. In 1873 the elected governor was *impeached*—accused of wrong-doing and removed from office—and Pinchback served as governor for forty-three days. P. B. S. Pinchback was born a slave in 1839, and he worked on a plantation in Mississippi. At the age of

Pinckney Benton Stewart Pinchback is the only Negro to ever serve as a state governor. He served as governor of Louisiana in 1873.

twelve he was given his freedom and went to work on the river boats on the Mississippi, Missouri, and Ohio rivers. During the Civil War he joined the Union Army and commanded a group of Negro soldiers from the state of Louisiana. P. B. S. Pinchback was a leader in the reorganization of the state government of Louisiana after the Civil War. Pinchback was later elected to the United States Senate. The Senate refused to give Pinchback his seat because the election was very close. It was disputed who had actually won the election. Pinchback therefore, never served in the United States Senate.

Booker T. Washington devoted his entire life to the building of Tuskegee Institute. He and his students built Tuskegee and raised much of their own food.

Robert B. Elliott was born free in Boston, Massachusetts in 1842. He was well educated at Eton school in London, England. He moved to South Carolina after the Civil War and became a leading political figure in that state. In 1868 he helped write the new state constitution of South Carolina. He served in the South Carolina legislature until 1870. Elliott was later elected to the United States Congress and he served in Congress with great distinction.

James and Patrick Healy were brothers who were born on a Georgia plantation in the 1830's. Both were to rise to important positions in the Roman Catholic Church. James graduated from Holy Cross College in 1849 and was ordained a priest in

Paris, France in 1854. He became the bishop of Portland, Maine in 1875. Patrick became a Jesuit priest and earned a Doctor of Philosophy degree from the University of Louvain in Belgium. He later became president of Georgetown University in Washington, D.C. from 1873 to 1882.

Who was Booker T. Washington?

Booker T. Washington is known today for the founding of Tuskegee Institute in Alabama. He was born in 1856 on a plantation in Virginia. His family moved to Malden, West Virginia after the Civil War. Young Booker T. Washington worked in the coal mines in Malden for ten to twelve hours a day. He wanted an education and went to school at night after working in the mines all day. From 1872 to 1875, he worked his way through Hampton Institute. This was a new school for Negroes in Virginia. He earned an excellent record at Hampton and in 1881 was asked to organize a new school for Negroes at Tuskegee, Alabama.

Booker T. Washington devoted the rest of his life to building Tuskegee Institute into a world famous school. The first classes were held in a broken-down church building. There were only thirty students and Washington was the only teacher. Washington and his students raised funds to buy land and building materials. They finally were able to buy an old run-down plantation. Washington and his students cleared the land of the old buildings and built new school buildings. Slowly they turned Tuskegee into a leading school. Booker T. Washington believed strongly in the value of hard work. He told his

students not to be ashamed to work with their hands. He said that honest labor was a great virtue. Tuskegee became outstanding as a school where Negroes could learn the skilled trades, such as bricklaying, building construction, and agriculture.

Washington worked hard to gain the cooperation of white people. He influenced the millionaire Andrew Carnegie to donate money to Tuskegee Institute. Washington believed that whites and Negroes could learn to respect each other and to live together peacefully. Booker T. Washington's favorite saying was "Cast down your bucket where you are." This meant that people should recognize their special problems and work hard to overcome them. The biggest problem for Negroes was to overcome the harmful effects of slavery. Negroes had to be taught how to help themselves rather than relying on others for help.

From its early days in an old wooden building, Tuskegee Institute has advanced to be one of the leading colleges in the country. This building is the Samuel Chapman Armstrong Hall where many science classess are held.

What were the contributions of George Washington Carver?

Increased educational opportunities for Negroes led to important accomplishments in science and technology. George Washington Carver was one of these scientists. He was born in Diamond Grove, Missouri in 1864. He left home when he was thirteen. He finished high school in Minneapolis, Kansas. Carver had a strong desire for more education and was determined to go to college. He entered Simpson College in Iowa when he was twenty-five years old. Carver remained only one year at Simpson College. One of Carver's teachers discovered he was interested in agriculture and helped him enter Iowa State College. In 1894 George Washington Carver became the first Negro to graduate from this school. He led his class in scholarship. Carver stayed at Iowa State College for two more years to do advanced research and to teach and study.

Booker T. Washington visited Iowa State College one day in 1896 and met Carver. He was impressed with Carver's intelligence. Booker T. Washington asked him to come to Tuskegee as a science teacher. Carver accepted this job offer and remained at Tuskegee until his death in 1943. Carver set up a laboratory at Tuskegee Institute, and from this laboratory came many great discoveries that changed the entire system of farming in the southern states.

Carver made many experiments with peanuts and discovered many useful products. From peanuts Carver made bleach, wood-filler, metal polish, paper, ink, rubbing oil, plastics and many other products. He experimented with sweet potatoes and learned to make starch, vinegar, rope, a type of rubber, and about one hundred other products. He also discovered that soybeans could be used to make flour and powered milk. He also learned many new ways to make plastics and dyes from wood shavings.

Southern farmers started to grow peanuts, soybeans, and sweet potatoes after these uses were discovered. They were a new source of income and prosperity for the entire South. Carver also taught farmers improved ways to fertilize the soil so more and better crops could be grown. Both white and Negro farmers were greatly aided by the discoveries of George Washington Carver.

Elijah McCoy, Jan Matzeliger, and Granville Woods were other famous Negro inventors during the years following slavery. From 1872 to 1920, McCoy invented many automatic lubricating appliances which were used on trains and steamships. Matzeliger created the first machine for attaching soles to shoes. This machine was patented in 1883 and helped make the production of shoes easier and faster. Woods gained patents on thirty-five different inventions from 1884 to 1910. His greatest inventions were an automatic air brake, which was manufactured by Westinghouse Company, and a Multiplex Railway Telegraph.

Who have been the great Afro-Americans of the twentieth century?

Afro-Americans have emerged during the twentieth century as leaders in science, music, politics, business, and sports.

Charles Richard Drew, Ernest Just, Percy Julian, and Theodore Lawless have led the way in science. Dr. Drew helped save many lives during World War II. He solved the problems of producing blood plasma from whole blood. He then became the first director of a project for collecting blood plasma for the American armed forces.

Dr. Just came from a poor family in South Carolina. He won a scholarship to Dartmouth College in New Hampshire. There he became interested in biology and the study of cell life. Later he taught biology at Howard University. While at Howard University he made many important discoveries about the structure and the reproduction of cells.

Dr. Percy Julian worked his way through DePauw University in Indiana. Today he is one of the most famous living Negro scientists. His greatest scientific contribution was the discovery of a drug to relieve pain caused by arthritis. Dr. Julian later founded a company to produce this and other drugs.

Dr. Theodore Lawless has become world famous for his medical discoveries. Dr. Lawless has made many important scientific contributions to the study of various skin diseases. Dr. Lawless has received the Harmon Award and many other awards and recognitions for his achievements.

POTATO

PEANUT

WALLBOARD

OIL PAINT

INK GLUE SHOE POLISH DYE DYNAMITE

Gwendolyn Brooks and Langston Hughes are two of the famous authors and poets of the 20th Century. Both Brooks and Hughes have received many awards and honors for their creative writing.

Who are some famous Negro artists, musicians, and athletes?

W. C. Handy, Charlie Parker, Louis Armstrong, and Duke Ellington have been leaders among the numerous brilliant Negro musicians. Jazz has become the most typical American form of music. It is a major contribution to the richness of American culture. Great Negro folksingers, such as Huddie Ledbetter, have added to the beauty and the variety of American music.

Langston Hughes, Ralph Ellison, Gwendolyn Brooks, and Richard Wright have been prize-winning Negro writers of the twentieth century. Langston Hughes has been writing outstanding poetry and plays since the 1920's. In 1959 he was honored with the Anisfield-Wolfe Award. His creativity has also earned him Rosenwald and Guggenheim awards. Ellison won the National Book Award in 1953 for his novel *Invisible Man*. Gwendolyn Brooks won the Pulitzer Prize for poetry in 1950. She has also won two Guggenheim Awards. Richard Wright's most famous book is *Native Son*. This book helped make Americans aware of the racial problems in the United States. Wright received the Guggenheim Award and also received the Spingarn Medal. Wright spent his last years in Paris, France where he died in 1960. Few writers have surpassed Wright in calling the attention of the world to the social problems in the U.S.

In the field of sports and entertainment Negroes continue to play leading roles. Willie Mays, Maury Wills, Jimmy Brown, Althea Gibson, Sydney Poitier, Sammy Davis, Jr., Harry Belafonte, Hank Aaron, and Jackie Robinson are only a few of the great Negro athletes and entertainers who are known to most Americans.

Who are some famous Negro public officials?

Numerous Negroes have had the chance to become political leaders during the past twenty-five years. Representative William Dawson of Chicago has played an important role in Congress. In 1949 Dawson became the first Negro to head a committee of Congress.

In 1961 Robert Weaver was named as head of the Housing and Home Finance Agency. Weaver later became the first Negro member of the President's Cabinet in 1966. He was named as the first Secretary of the new Department of Housing and Urban Affairs.

In 1965 Thurgood Marshall, the famous NAACP lawyer, was named as Solicitor General for the United States. Marshall has built an impressive record as a lawyer, and some people have called him the greatest constitutional lawyer of the twentieth century. In 1967 Thurgood Marshall was appointed to the Supreme Court. He was the first Negro to ever serve on the United States

Many public officials, such as Carl Stokes, were elected to office by the common support of both white and Negro voters.

Supreme Court.

Other Negroes have won important political positions in the past few years. Edward Brooke was elected Senator from the state of Massachusetts. Carl Stokes was elected mayor of the city of Cleveland, Ohio. And Richard Hatcher was elected mayor of the city of Gary, Indiana. All three of these men were elected only with the combined support of both white and Negro voters.

143

William Edward Burghardt DuBois helped found the Niagara Movement and the National Association for the Advancement of Colored People.

What have been the contributions of W. E. B. DuBois?

William Edward Burghardt DuBois was born in Massachusetts in 1868. He graduted from Fisk University, Harvard University, and attended the University of Berlin in Germany. He was a professor at Wilburforce University and the University of Pennsylvania. While at the University of Pennsylvania he wrote a brilliant study of the way of life of Negroes in a large city. This book is called *The Philadelphia Negro*. Later he taught at Atlanta University where he continued his studies of

Negro life. He wrote *The Souls of Black Folk* in which he cried out against the unfair treatment of American Negroes.

W. E. B. DuBois began to openly criticize Booker T. Washington. DuBois admired Washington as a great leader and a hard worker but disagreed with some of his views. He disagreed with Washington's belief that Negroes should stay out of politics. Washington thought Negroes should prepare themselves for farming and skilled trades. DuBois said these ideas of Washington's condemned Negroes to second class citizenship. DuBois believed that intelligent Negroes should become doctors, lawyers, businessmen and politicians. Above all DuBois believed Negroes should become involved in government and politics in order to win political power. He said only through the wide use of political power by Negroes could segregation be completely destroyed.

DuBois stressed organization and strong protest as methods to end segregation and gain political power for Negroes. W. E. B. DuBois helped organize the Niagara Movement. The Niagara Movement later grew into the National Association for the Advancement of Colored People. In 1957 DuBois decided to leave the United States. He became a citizen of Ghana in western Africa. He died there in Ghana in 1963 at the age of ninety-five.

What have been the contributions of Martin Luther King, Jr.?

Martin Luther King, Jr. has been the most famous civil rights leader of the 1960's. He was the son of a Baptist minister and was exposed to books and ideas from the time he was a child. He received a good education and earned degrees from Morehouse college, Crozer Theological Seminary, and Boston University.

In college King became interested in the books of Mohandas Gandhi. Gandhi was the leader of India's struggle to win independence from Great Britain. King was influenced by the gentle character of Gandhi and the effectiveness of Gandhi's non-violent methods of protest. This non-violent protest is called *passive resistence*. King realized that the ideas of passive resistence agreed with the ideas of Christianity in the Bible. King believed that non- violent protest would be the key to the Negro struggle for civil rights. He said if Negroes refused to use violence when insulted or attacked, the attackers who used violence would be shown as hateful and undesirable people. King's ideas have worked many times. The violence used against King's marchers in Birmingham, Alabama helped influence Congress to pass the Civil Rights Act of 1964. The attacks on civil rights marchers in Selma, Alabama in 1965 helped win support for the Voting Rights Act of 1965.

King was awarded the Nobel Peace Prize in 1964 in recognition of his peaceful protest methods. He was the second American Negro to receive this high award. Ralph Bunche received the Nobel Peace Prize in 1950 for his work for the United Nations in settling the Arab-Israeli War.

Dr. Martin Luther King's career in the struggle for civil rights was ended April 4, 1968. Dr. King, the leader of the non-violent civil rights movement, was murdered in Memphis, Tennessee. The entire nation mourned the loss of this great man.

The careers of all of the great American Negroes show that America has sometimes been a land of struggle, strife, and hardship for Negroes. The careers of these great people also show that America has sometimes been a land of equal opportunity and achievement.

Gandhi's idea of passive resistance was used by Martin Luther King, Jr., as a method of non-violent protest.

Knowing Your Vocabulary

almanac /'ȯl-mə-ˌnak/
A book that gives the days of the week, ideas for improved farming, business ideas, puzzles, and astronomical happenings. 131

passive resistence /'pas-iv ri-'zis-tən(t)s/

The method of non-violent protest against something a group of people think is wrong. 145

impeach /im-'pēch/
To be accused of wrong-doing and removed from a political office. 137

Reading the Text

1. Explain how the idea of passive resistence can be effectively used?

2. Why do you think Martin Luther King, Jr. adopted the idea of passive resistence?

3. Do you agree with W. E. B. DuBois' idea that Negroes should prepare themselves for professions and political power? What are your reasons for agreeing or disagreeing?

4. What are some of the reasons why people like Rilleux, Wright, and DuBois left the United States to live in another country?

5. What is the importance of the recent elections of Brooke, Stokes, and Hatcher?

6. How did the discoveries of George Washington Carver change the system of farming in the southern states?

7. Why did Negroes during the time of slavery have a difficult time making progress? During Reconstruction? During the era of segregation? Today?

8. In your opinion, which one of the people mentioned in this chapter has made the greatest contribution to American life? What are your reasons for selecting this one person?

9. In your opinion, which one of the people mentioned in this chapter has made the greatest contribution to Negro civil rights and the ending of segregation in the United States? What are your reasons for selecting this one person?

Identifying Names and Places

Benjamin Banneker
Phillis Wheatley
James Derham
Lemuel Haynes
Joshua Bishop
Prince Hall
Absalom Jones
Richard Allen
Frederick Douglass
Harriet Tubman
Sojourner Truth
Norbert Rilleux
Paul Cuffe
James Forten
Blanche K. Bruce
Robert Smalls
P. B. S. Pinchback
Robert Elliott
James Healy
Patrick Healy
Booker T. Washington
George Washington Carver
Elijah McCoy
Jan Matzeliger
Granville Woods
Charles Richard Drew
Ernest Just
Percy Julian
W. C. Handy
Louis Armstrong
Charlie Parker
Langston Hughes
Ralph Ellison
Gwendolyn Brooks
Richard Wright
Robert Weaver
Thurgood Marshall
W. E. B. DuBois
Martin Luther King, Jr.

Debating and Discussing Ideas

1. Which method has been most successful in ending segregation? Is it the method of Booker T. Washington, W. E. B. DuBois, or Martin Luther King, Jr.? Why has this method been the most successful?

2. How do civil rights organizations today hope to accomplish their goals? Will these methods be successful?

Reading Other Sources

Adams, Russell F., *Great Negroes Past and Present*, Chicago: Afro-Am, 1963.

Graham, Shirley and Lipscomb, George, *Dr. George Washington Carver*, New York: Messner, 1944.

Hughes, Langston, *Famous American Negroes*, New York: Dodd, Mead, 1954.

Kugelmoss, J. A., *Ralph J. Bunche: Fighter for Peace*, New York: Messner, 1952.

Richardson, Ben Albert, *Great American Negroes*, New York: Crowell, 1956.

Yates, Elizabeth, *Amos Fortune: Free Man*, New York: Dutton, 1950.

7. Toward The Future

I have a dream that one day
on the red hills of Georgia
the sons of former slaves
and the sons of former slave owners
will be able to sit down together
at the table of brotherhood . . . .

Martin Luther King, Jr.

American Negroes have made great progress during the one hundred years since the end of slavery. They have had to overcome many difficulties in order to make this progress. They have had to take advantage of every opportunity opened to them. Many times these opportunities were very few. They had to struggle constantly to gain new rights and opportunities. Often the struggle was hard and many times was unsuccessful. As the years passed a growing number of white people have taken part in the struggle for Negro progress. This cooperation between white and Negro people is an outstanding example of American democracy at work. The fact that Negroes have achieved so much through peaceful, gradual, and legal means and methods is an example to the world that American democracy does work to solve the many problems and protests of a minority group.

This record of progress does not mean that most Negroes are satisfied with their present role and status in American society. It does not mean that Negroes no longer suffer from injustices and unequal treatment. It does not mean that Negroes no longer suffer from white violence, racial discrimination, and segregation in the United States. But no one can deny that American Negroes have progressed a long way since the days of slavery. Hopefully greater progress will be made in the years ahead.

The educational and economic progress of Negroes will hopefully continue at a rapid pace. Recent laws from the federal, state, and local governments have opened new opportunities for Negroes. As Negroes take advantage of these new opportunities, the role and status of Negroes in American society will improve more and more. In the years ahead, if segregation disappears, with it will disappear the low status and role of the Negro.

If the Negro people achieve full integration into all areas of American life, they will then vote as naturally and easily as other Americans. Schools and jobs in all parts of the country will be open to them. Many more Negroes will rise to positions of national leadership and importance. The ability of individual Negroes, not their race or color, will determine how far they progress. This will indeed fulfill the prophesy of Martin Luther King, Jr. that he made on August 28, 1963, when he spoke to the demonstrators during the march on Washington. He said, "I have a dream that one day on the red hills of Georgia the sons of former slaves and the sons of former slave owners will be able to sit down together at the table of brotherhood. ... I have a dream that my four little children will one day live in a nation where they will not be judged by the color of their skins but by the content of their character."

Every person in the United States has an important stake in the fulfillment of Reverend King's dream of racial integration and cooperation. The fulfillment of this dream would bring an end to racial hatred—the dislike of a man merely because he looks different. Our nation could only benefit from the fulfillment of Reverend King's dream. Blind hatred hurts those who are hated and destroys the personality of those who hate. The fulfillment of this dream would bring an end to racial riots and violence. And our nation could only benefit from an end to the destruction of property and the loss of life.

The fulfillment of this dream would allow the United States to present to the world an example of cooperation and harmony and peace. And our nation gains strength when all our citizens cooperate instead of fighting one another.

When Negroes achieve complete integration into American society, they will have proved some important things to themselves, to other Americans, and to the world. They will have proved that American democracy is more than just words about freedom and the rights of man. They will have proved to all people of the world that the United States

In some areas of American life, Dr. King's dream has come true. Public beaches, amusement parks, and other recreational facilities are no longer segregated.

Racial peace and equality begins with the young.

of America still has a message about freedom and human dignity to which all nations should listen. Americans will have proved that people of different types and races can live together in peace and equality.

The goals of the Civil Rights Movement are to gain the complete rewards and duties of citizenship in the United States.

151

Summary of Major Ideas

The story of how Afro-Americans have progressed in America is full of lessons about the meaning of courage, struggle, achievement, and democracy. This story shows how Afro-Americans have progressed and have contributed greatly to the progress of the United States of America. These people have worked from the lowly position of slavery to the dignity of freedom and equality.

Historical methods are a way to learn about the past by carefully examining historical documents.

Five steps can be followed when you are using historical methods to study documents. The first step is to find out who wrote the document, when the document was written, and where the document was written. The second step is to find out what facts and what opinions are stated in the document. The third step is to discover why the facts in the document are important. The fourth step is to make conclusions about past events. These conclusions should be based upon the facts that are stated in the documents. The fifth step is to identify new questions about the past that are raised by the document.

Throughout the history of the United States of America, most Afro-Americans have remained at the bottom levels of society or had a lower status than most white people in America.

The position or status of most Afro-Americans has been lower than the position or status of most white people throughout America's past history. Most black Americans were slaves until the Emancipation Proclamation and the Thirteenth Amendment. The role of the slave was to behave as an inferior person when he was around white people. A slave was expected to work hard, to always be obedient and loyal to the master, and to behave as if all white people were superior to all black people. After 1865, segregation was used to keep the Afro-Americans at the lower levels of society. Because of segregation, black people were deprived of equal opportunities to get an education, to get a job, or to vote. Compared to most white people, black people had less money, poorer homes, and poorer health. Segregation, like slavery, forced Afro-Americans to behave as inferior people. Segregation was a solid barrier against the improvement of the status and role of most Afro-Americans.

White racism has been the main reason why most Afro-Americans have remained at the bottom levels of American society.

Racism is the belief that one race is naturally superior to other races. Scientists tell us that racism is a false idea. These scientists say that all races have the same ability to make progress, and that all races have contributed to human progress and civilization. People of great ability and people of little ability may be found among all racial groups. However, many white people have been racists. Because these whites have believed that all black people are naturally inferior, they have also believed that black people should not live as well as white people. These racist beliefs have prevented Afro-Americans from having the same rights and opportunities enjoyed by most white people. Afro-Americans have been kept from having equal rights to vote, to hold public office, to get a job, to become educated, to receive medical care, or to live where they want to live.

Many Afro-Americans have reacted with either passive indifference, silent hatred, or violent protest against the American society that has restricted the equality, opportunity, and freedom of the Afro-American.

Many black people came to believe that they really were inferior to whites because of the inferior roles and statuses forced upon them during slavery and segregation. Many accepted their lowly position in life. Other Afro-Americans reacted violently to the laws of slavery and segregation. Slave revolts and riots were the first protests against white racism. After the end of slavery, some Afro-Americans organized self-help groups to win and to protect their rights. Many organizations such as the NAACP and the Urban League have struggled to win civil rights for Negroes. This struggle for civil rights has, for the most part, been conducted peacefully. Violence, however, has sometimes broken out when Afro-Americans have lashed out in bitterness at a society that has denied them full opportunity and freedom. During the past twenty years, the segregation system and white racism has been breaking down. More and more black Americans have rejected their old status and role of inferiority. The future of America will depend on whether all Americans will be willing to let a person's ability decide his status and role in life rather than his skin color.

PRONUNCIATION SYMBOLS

By permission. From Webster's Seventh New Collegiate Dictionary, copyright 1967 by G. & C. Merriam Company, publishers of the Merriam-Webster Dictionaries.

a as in map	i as in tip	s as in less
ā as in day	ī as in side	sh as in shy
ä as in cot	j as in job	t as in tie
à as in father	k as in kin	th as in thin
aù as in out	l as in pool	t͟h as in then
b as in baby	m as in dim	ü as in rule
ch as in chin	n as in no	ù as in pull
d as in did	ŋ as in sing	v as in give
e as in bed	ō as in bone	w as in we
ē as in easy	ȯ as in saw	y as in yard
f as in cuff	ȯi as in coin	z as in zone
g as in go	p as in lip	zh as in vision
h as in hat	r as in rarity	ə as in banana, collect

Glossary

The words pronounced and defined below are those words italicized and defined in the text. The numbers indicate the pages on which the words are first defined.

Abolition Movement /ˌab-ə-ˈlish-ən ˈmüv-mənt/ A group of people who joined together to end slavery in the United States. 42

almanac /ˈȯl-mə-ˌnak/ Books that give the days of the week, ideas for improved farming, business ideas, puzzles, and astronomical happenings. 131

amendment /ə-ˈmen(d)-mənt/ An addition to the Constitution of the United States of America. 62

appeal /ə-ˈpē(ə)l/ To have a criminal or civil case heard again by a higher court. 80

assassinate /ə-ˈsas-ən-ˌāt/ The murder of a high government official or other public figure. 63

boycott /ˈbȯi-ˌkät/ The refusal by a group of people to buy certain products or to use certain services. 107

carpetbagger /ˈkär-pət-bag-ər/ A northerner who came to the South during the Reconstruction era. 65

caste /ˈkast/ A group or class of people that are kept apart from other groups or classes of people. 90

Caucasoid /ˈkȯ-kə-ˌsȯid/ One of the three main racial groups of people in the world. 22

centennial /sen-ˈten-ē-əl/ The anniversary one hundred years after an event. 109

chronological order /ˌkrän-əl-ˈäj-i-kəl ˈȯrd-ər/ Placing past events in the order in which they happened. 11

civil rights /ˈsiv-əl-rīts/ The full rights, duties, and rewards of citizenship in the United States. 9

Civil Rights Revolution /ˈsiv-əl rīts ˌrev-ə-ˈlü-shən/ The name given to the demonstrations for Negro civil rights during the 1960's. 110

conclusion /kən-ˈklü-zhən/ The individual judgment of a person about a question or issue after studying the facts. 13

Congressional Medal of Honor /ˈkäŋ-grəs-shən-əl-ˈmed-əl-əv-ˈän-ər/ The highest military award that is given by the United States. 46

cotton gin /ˈkät-ən-ˈjin/ A machine invented by Eli Whitney to separate the seeds from the cotton fibers. 36

document /'däk-yə-,ment/ A written record of what men have said, done, or seen in the past. 10

Emancipation Proclamation /i-,man(t)-sə-'pā-shən-,präk-lə-'mā-shən/ A document issued by President Abraham Lincoln that freed all slaves living in the states rebelling against the federal government in 1863. 46

fact /'fakt/ Something that an individual can be quite certain is absolutely true. 12

fair employment practices law /'fa(ə)r im-'plȯi-mənt 'prak-təs-əs 'lȯ/ Laws that protect all people against unfair treatment and discrimination when they apply for jobs. 106

field slaves /'fē(ə)ld 'slāv/ Slaves that did the heavy farm work on the plantations and farms of the South. 38

Freedman's Bureau /'frēd-məns 'byu̇-(ə)r-(,)ō/ An agency of the federal government organized to help Negroes after their emancipation. 61

median /'mēd-ē-ən/ The amount of something where one-half of the total population is higher, and one-half is lower. 85

Middle Passage /'mid-əl 'pas-ij/ The name given to the crossing of the Atlantic Ocean by the ships carrying slaves to the New World. 35

migrate /'mī-,grāt/ When a large group of people move to another area of the earth. 23

militia /mə-'lish-ə/ A local or state army, usually called upon during times of public emergencies. 41

Mongoloid /'mäŋ-gə-,lȯid/ One of the three main racial groups in the world. 22

Negroid /'nē-,grȯid/ One of the three main ·racial groups of people in the world. 22

open occupancy law /'ō-pən 'äk-yə-pən-se 'lȯ/ Laws that give every person the right to buy or rent homes in any section of a city. 116

opinion /ə-'pin-yən/ An individual judgment or belief about something. 12

overseer /'ō-və(r)-,si(ə)r/ A man hired to be the boss ȯf a group of slave workers. 38

pardon /'pärd-ən/ A release from the penalty of a jail sentence or fine. 63

passive resistence /'pas-iv ri-'zis-tən(t)s/ The method of non-violent protest against something that a group of people think is wrong. 145

planter /'plant-ər/ Rich farm owners in the South before the Civil War. 36

poll tax /'pōl-'taks/ A tax or a money payment that was collected by the states before a person was allowed to vote. 81

primary source /'prī-,mer-ē 'sō(ə)rs/ The original or first-hand source of historical information. 10

racism /'rā-,siz-əm/ A belief in the natural superiority of one race over all other races. 19

rebellion /ri-'bel-yən/ A violent uprising to overthrow the power of the people who are presently ruling. 39

role /'rōl/ The actions that a person is expected to perform. 49

scalawag /'skal-i-,wag/ A southerner who cooperated with federal officials during the era of Reconstruction. 65

secondary source /'sek-ən-,der-ē 'sō(ə)rs/ Sources of information that are not the original or first-hand source. 10

segregation /,seg-ri-'gā-shən/ The practice of separating Negroes and whites in the United States. 79

sharecropper /'she(ə)r-,kräp-ər/ A person who farms land owned by someone else. Rent is paid by giving the owner a share of the crop produced. 69

sit-in /'sit-in/ A group of people sitting in a place of business so that no one else can be served. It is used as a method to end segregation. 108

slavery /'slāv-(ə)-rē/ When a group of people have no freedom and are under the control of other people. 31

status /'stat-əs/ The rank or position a person holds among the people with whom he lives. 47

Underground Railroad /'ən-dər-ˌgraůnd 'rā(ə)l-ˌrōd/ The many escape routes that were used by slaves fleeing the South before the Civil War. 43

veto /'vēt-(ˌ)ō/ An objection to a law by the President of the United States. 64

INDEX

Words found here in boldface type will also be found in the Glossary, where explanation and pronunciation are given.

ACKNOWLEDGMENTS

Acknowledgment is made to the following for permission to reproduce photographs.

Abbey Aldrich Rockefeller Folk Art Collection, 50
Bettmann Archive, 11, 44 (top), 46, 64-65, 71, 84 (top), 85
Chicago Public School Photo, 148
Culver Pictures Service, 26 (bottom), 40 (left), 62 (bottom), 63 (bottom), 66 (top), 70, 82 (top), 137, 139
Field Museum of Natural History, Sculptress—Malvina Hoffman, 18, 24-25
Greensboro News Record, 119 (bottom left)
Historical Picture Service, 30, 38, 40 (right), 41, 49 (bottom), 62 (top), 63 (top), 66 (bottom), 119 (top), 132
Minneapolis Tribune, 119 (bottom right)
New York Times, 12-13, 87-89
Philadelphia Convention Bureau, 148
UPI, 10, 20 (bottom), 23 (right), 26 (top), 82 (bottom), 83, 84 (bottom), 104, 107, 110 (bottom), 113, 115-116, 142-143, 145, 150
Wide World Photos, 2 (top), 2 (middle), 23 (left and middle), 90, 102, 105-106, 108, 110 (top), 111, 112, 144, 151

ARTISTS

Michael Davis, Title page, 8, 14, 21-22, 32-37, 39, 42-43, 45, 47-48, 51 (top), 60, 68-69, 78, 80, 86, 104, 109, 130, 133-136, 138, 141
C. F. Horndorf, Chapter end symbols
Donald Meighan, Cover Design
James Teason, Cover Artist
Berthold Tiedemann, 49 (top), 117